Treasure in the Cellar

by Steven Otfinoski

◆

illustrated by
Beth Peck

Scott Foresman

Editorial Offices: Glenview, Illinois • New York, New York
Sales Offices: Reading, Massachusetts • Duluth, Georgia
Glenview, Illinois • Carrollton, Texas • Menlo Park, California

NARRATOR: It is a beautiful Saturday morning. Puffy billows of white clouds fill the blue sky. Ben is coming up the steps from his cellar. Billows of dust come up from the basement with him. He is carrying a pile of old newspapers. His friend Tom walks by. Ben bellows a loud hello.

BEN: Hello, Tom! Where are you going?

TOM: I'm going to play basketball over at Mike's house. Do you want to come along?

BEN: Thanks. But I'm busy.

Tom: It looks as if you're stuck cleaning out your cellar. What a way to spend a Saturday!

Ben: Oh, I'm not cleaning. I'm hunting.

Tom: Hunting for what?

Ben: For treasure!

Tom: Ben, what are you talking about?

Ben: It's a long story.

Tom: Go ahead. I'm listening.

BEN: Well, my Uncle Albert was an explorer. He discovered a tomb in Egypt.

TOM: A tomb with a mummy in it?

BEN: That's right. And there was treasure in the tomb too. Uncle Albert gave most of it to a museum. But Dad says he kept the best thing for himself.

TOM: What is it doing in your cellar?

BEN: When Uncle Albert died, all his things came to our house. We put them in the cellar. My Dad says if I can find the treasure in all his stuff, it's mine.

TOM: Wow! That's great!

BEN: Well, I'd better get back to work. The cellar is loaded with junk. I've got to take it all out to find the treasure.

TOM: Ben, you have a big job ahead of you. Would you like some help?

BEN: But I thought you were going to play basketball.

TOM: Oh, I can play basketball anytime.

BEN: That's a great offer, Tom. But I wouldn't want you to work for nothing.

TOM: Well, what if we split any treasure we find? That would be fair, wouldn't it?

BEN: I guess so. Okay, Tom. If we find the treasure, we'll split it.

TOM: Great! Let's get to work!

NARRATOR: For two hours, Tom and Ben drag everything out of the cellar. They find old furniture, dusty boxes, and a stuffed bird with tufts of feathers. More dust billows up. They put the worthless things by the curb. They put the other things back in the cellar.

Tom: I don't get it, Ben. We didn't find any treasure, just this picture of a guy. Who do you think he is?

Ben: It's Uncle Albert! Look at those tufts of white hair under his hat!

Tom: Don't tell me this is the treasure?

Ben: Well, it could be. Uncle Albert had a funny sense of humor.

TOM: But you said we'd find real treasure.

BEN: Well, Uncle Albert did like to tell tall tales. Maybe he made up the part about the treasure.

TOM: Or maybe his nephew did! Did you make up this whole treasure story to get me to help you clean your cellar?

NARRATOR: At that moment, Mr. Brown, Ben's dad, bellows a hello from the doorway. Then he comes outside.

MR. BROWN: It looks as if you guys did a great job cleaning!

BEN: Thanks, Dad. I couldn't have done it without Tom.

MR. BROWN: Good for you, Tom. It's nice to see friends helping each other. Here's the ten dollars I promised. Five for each of you.

NARRATOR: Mr. Brown then hands each boy a five-dollar bill. Tom looks surprised and very pleased.

TOM: Thanks, Mr. Brown!

MR. BROWN: Thank you, Tom. You can put that picture of Uncle Albert out with the other trash. We have much better pictures of him.

NARRATOR: Mr. Brown goes back inside the house.

TOM: So much for your treasure!

BEN: But you did get five dollars, didn't you?

TOM: That's the part I can't figure out. Why didn't you just tell me your dad would pay me for helping, instead of telling me that crazy treasure story?

BEN: If I had told you, would you have helped me?

NARRATOR: Tom thinks for a moment. Then he
bellows out a laugh.

TOM: No, I guess I wouldn't have. It was the
treasure that caught my interest. But now I'm glad
to have the five dollars.

NARRATOR: The two friends shake hands. Then Ben
picks up the picture of Uncle Albert.

15

Tom: If you don't mind, I'd like that picture.

Ben: What for?

Tom: It just might come in handy when I have to clean out my cellar. I know some other guys who might be interested in going on a "treasure hunt" too.

Narrator: The two friends laugh.

THE END

Barefoot

Baylis Glascock

birchwoodpress.com

In memory of Peter and Frances Yates

ISBN: 978-0-9965153-9-9 (paperback)
ISBN: 978-1-7378065-0-9 (e-book)

Library of Congress Control Number: 2021949106

Author photo: Aaron Glascock
Copyeditor: Lois Smith, loiswordsmithunlimited.com;
    additional copyediting by Roberta Goodwin
Cover art: Sarah Glascock
Cover design: Karen Quagletti, karenq.com

Published in the USA by
Birchwood Press
Los Angeles, CA
http://www.birchwoodpress.com
birchwoodpress@gmail.com

Table of Contents

The Farm

My childhood was not without good moments. It is perhaps
the nature of the growing child to simply make the best of
what may be given. And for all that I might have lacked
or later thought I lacked, I did have the farm. The piece of
land that seemed to have been there forever and that I was
free to roam as often as I wanted.

In winter, though, I wore extra layers of clothing, never
really feeling warm enough. But I marveled at the absolute beauty of ice covering the trees. Coating every twig
and blade of grass. And when the sun shone, I could walk
through the small pasture that lay between the house and
the dairy barn and see, among the blades of dead grass,
among the tiny divots and rivulets in the snow, a vast
terrain of hills and canyons traversed by my own tiny
railroad. A railroad with bridges and trestles of immense
complexity. The trip from house to barn, a mere three
hundred yards, could take the better part of an hour.

Or I could walk near the highway along the fence in the
early and brief winter sunset and listen to the crackle of ice
under my feet. Clapping my hands, I could hear the sound
strike the power lines and ricochet along them into the
distance, a phenomenon that filled me with awe. Again and
again I clapped my hands to hear that strange doppler.

In the summer, there could be cloudbursts. An inch or
more of rain in five or six minutes. All the space around a
wall of water. Once, when we were in the family car, it was
necessary to pull off the road and stop. When we got home,

the rain had ceased, and every surface was alive with flowing water: the road, the fields, the ditches. My brother and I ran barefooted through the grass and mud, following the flow of water. Our whole farm magically transformed into a realm of streams and tiny waterfalls. A place for splashing and throwing rocks. A place for yelling at the sky, a place of unbounded joy.

The woods were thicker then, with a dense blackberry patch not far north of the abandoned short-line track. No track left, just the roadbed. In the low places were concrete culverts six or eight feet wide, the ceilings caked with colonies of mud-dauber wasps. And on the walls, the mud nests of swallows. My brothers and I rested there on hot summer days. But often I came to the woods alone. I loved the mosses that thrived at the bases of trees. The occasional tiny flower.

"That's a jack in the pulpit," Mom said as we walked together once. There it was, delicate and alone under the canopy of trees in a shaft of afternoon light, a jewel to be left as it was found. Sometimes we would hunt mushrooms, Mom and I. Morels. Finding one here, one there. And once, dozens and dozens in a small area no bigger than the back porch.

On the fence at the northeast edge of the farm was a solitary gooseberry bush. It stood there unbothered in the fence line, waiting for the birds to enjoy its fruit.

If you climbed the silo, you could see trees and hedgerows, fields, houses and barns of neighboring farms, all in one sweep, the breeze blowing in your face. The smell of rotting silage and manure ascending the shaft. From this

height, the surrounding ground seemed to revolve, the
Earth to spread out in all directions. The tall silos looming
over barn and milk parlor, feedlot, and bullpen. Something
ancient, forbidding, and mysterious. Once functional, now
standing like blind lighthouses, sightless beacons to those
passing on the highway, ploughing in a distant field. A
roosting place for pigeons.

This land at the edge of the prairie. This small farm in
the center of the country was the center of my father's
world, as it had been for his father and grandfather. Land
that had succored generations of my family. Land they had
served, as it had served them. Clearing, planting, harvest-
ing, fertilizing, always demanding toil. In good times, the
land gave bountifully. Its true wealth, a place to be. A place
to live in communion with nature. This communion, the
very ground of their being. Understood deeply, but they had
no words for it. As if, like the true name of God, it could
not be spoken.

The Road West

The road leading west from town had been paved in 1934. State Highway 19, a concrete slab bisected by a stripe of black tar and segmented at fifty-foot intervals so that tires made a kathump-kathump traveling over it. Dad's car moved toward his house almost as though it knew the way, a mere two miles that Dad had walked hundreds of times going to and from school as a boy. He had traveled it on horseback, in buggies, on hay wagons, on tractors pulling combines, in trucks loaded with grain. The road was a part of him like the cartilage between his bones. He knew the road, its inclines and curves, the way a musician knows music: without thinking of the piece as a whole, when a part of a melody is sung, the succeeding notes come forth as needed.

Our farm appeared on the right at the top of a small rise. "This field is the highest ground in the county," Dad said as he rode the tractor with me one day. The fields and the boundaries of the farm were defined by fences, woven wire fences on wood posts, with two strands of barbed wire on top. Dad had built plenty of fences. That was a basic farming skill. It was work that I did helping my Uncle Harry one summer. Dad said that good fences were basic to farming. They had to be built well and maintained. Dad tended to be generous and forgiving but seemed to remember when people had tried to take advantage of him or renege on an agreement. There were people who had difficulty remembering their promises. Fences were shared responsibilities.

Each farmer was responsible for building and maintaining half the length of the fence between them, the half on the right as viewed from his own field.

Our house was a simple structure. Dad had been born in it in 1909. His parents had come to the house directly from their wedding in Perry, eighteen miles to the west. The short-line railroad crossed the length of the farm from east to west, and they'd had the train stop right there in the middle of the farm and had gotten off and walked the three hundred yards to the house in their wedding clothes. The house was surrounded by elm trees and pasture, with several small sheds, a smokehouse, and a horse feed barn behind. Dad often talked about how his Aunt Betty had spent her final months in that very house in the summer of 1924 as she was dying of throat cancer.

His mother had cared for Aunt Betty until her death. The house was full of memories of his childhood and teen years. Memories of the meals cooked on the wood stove in the kitchen. Thousands of meals had been cooked in that kitchen. Dad always bragged about Grandma's sourdough biscuits. Always a jar of clabber, sour milk, in the kitchen kept just for making biscuits. He would brag that she never used a recipe, never seemed to measure the ingredients. They were simply without compare, he would say.

Dad was a person given to superlatives. There was a cousin in Detroit who was a theater organist. "Best in the world, no one like her," he would say. There was his friend George, who could outrun just about anybody even in full football gear and uniform. There was a famous relative named Al the Answer Man, had a radio program for White Owl cigars. "Could answer absolutely any question. No one ever stumped him. It was just uncanny," Dad would say. Dad's friend Razor was one hell of a carpenter, though Razor always smelled of whiskey and had blazing red eyes. Dad would brag that his friend W. L. was a national skeet champion for three consecutive years. Dad had a generally high estimation of his friends, men with extraordinary abilities. "Charles Lemon was as good a judge of cattle as you could find anywhere." Except for Charles, most of Dad's friends liked a good drink of whiskey now and then.

Dad didn't smoke, never did, and was proud of it. Granddad had given him a gold watch for not drinking or smoking until he was twenty-one. But after that he more than made up for the drinking he had not done before. I wasn't aware of Dad's drinking until about the time I was in the first or second grade. Mom never understood what it was that made Dad drink. She cooked supper every night, but often we would eat without him. As we got older we would hear him come home late at night.

At 5:30 a.m. Dad would rise in the dark, shower and shave, pat his cheeks with Old Spice aftershave lotion, comb his hair with Wildroot Cream Oil, don a starched white shirt and tie, suit, overcoat, and galoshes, and be out the door without a word. Mom would have a couple of hours rest without Dad's snoring.

Outside Dad starts the Hudson, lets it run for a couple of minutes to warm up. The exhaust glows red in the dark, chill air illuminated by the taillights. Dad slowly eases the massive gray Hudson onto the highway and cautiously navigates the ice-coated road toward town. He glances to light beaming from his dairy barn, two hundred yards off the highway and standing out in the darkness like a beacon on a distant shore. Frank, the hired hand, is already milking the herd of thirty-two Guernseys.

In the back of the post office, rural carriers were already sorting mail for their routes. There was a big stack of Sears Roebuck catalogs for each carrier. The smell of two new tires to be delivered to Albert Scott, R.R. #3, permeated the room. A radio played country music and would soon be giving the cattle and hog market prices and corn, oat, and wheat prices. By 7:00 the rural carriers were gone, and Dad and his clerk would finish putting up the mail in the lobby boxes. At 8:00 a.m. the window would open for the day's business.

The post office in a small town is a vector of information. Letters, postcards, parcels, publications, money orders, bank statements, notices: working in the post office, Dad knows a lot about each person who comes and goes through the lobby door. But he regards his position as a public trust and does not traffic in tidbits of gossip gleaned from this flow of data, nor does he permit his clerks to do so. He is not stiff or prudish about it. He simply follows official Post Office policy, thinking it is plain good sense.

Granddad

When I was three, Grandma and Granddad Glascock moved from the farm to town. For a while, they lived in a house that belonged to Uncle Tubby and Aunt Lucy. That was during the war. Uncle Tubby and Aunt Lucy had moved to Kansas City, where Uncle Tubby had a job.

The back porch on the other side of the house had an awning with large dark green stripes and small orange stripes. The awning could roll up to be out of the way or rolled down to make shade. This was the only awning in town. It seemed more important and interesting than any other part of a house I had ever seen. On the living room wall of that house was a large framed print: a scene of a wolf howling in the winter night with a log cabin in the valley below. I looked at it for a long time. It was a lonely picture, and it bothered me. What were the people in the house doing? Was the wolf going to eat them?

It was a dark winter night when I stayed one evening with Granddad while Mom and Dad went somewhere to a club meeting. Grandma must have gone too, because she wasn't home. Granddad sat in his big rocking chair reading a newspaper under his reading lamp. He was barefooted, and the nail of the big toe on his left foot was split down the middle. It looked just like a cow's hoof. For some reason I couldn't understand, he was teasing me with the toe. He would reach out with his foot and pinch me with the toes of his left foot. It hurt. He did this several times.

Granddad

The only toy in the house was a metal Greyhound bus, large and sturdy enough that I could sit on top. I rode it back and forth in the living room. Granddad didn't talk to me or read to me. He just read the paper to himself. The rest of the house was dark. The only light was his reading lamp.

In the summer, my half-brother, Stevie, would visit Granddad and Grandma. Sometimes I would go to Granddad's to play with Stevie. This was during the war, and there were cut-out toy military vehicles on the back of Kix cereal boxes. One afternoon, Stevie and I played in the yard in the grass with some of them. A cardboard tank, a jeep, and a howitzer. We placed them on a large sheet of paper with the layout of a military base, which came inside the box as a premium. A large bug crawled from the grass onto the paper and waddled across in front of the tank.

I went with Stevie up the street to Careverly Ann Scott's house that afternoon. She had her own room in the garage. It was her childhood clubhouse, she said, and two of her friends were there with her. She had a small keg of hot, flat ginger beer. She offered me a cup. I was thirsty, but it tasted awful. I was so disappointed. They all laughed.

From Granddad's house it was only a block up to the Christian Church where I went to Sunday school every week. Granddad never missed Sunday school, and neither did I. Granddad was an elder, and if we stayed for church services, I would see him go to the front of the church with the other elders to serve communion. I was little then, so I didn't get any of the grape juice or the cracker. When I was a little older, I went to the church with Granddad on a weekday afternoon. There were wasps making a nest over one of the main doors. Granddad made a torch with a roll of newspaper and tore down the nest. One of the wasps stung him. "Darn," he said, "that hurt." Granddad never said bad words.

One morning, I walked uptown with Granddad, past the courthouse to the home of one of his friends, another old man. He and his friend talked. I could not tell what they were talking about. I wiggled my foot. Finally, his friend turned to a large desk with drawers and pulled out a wooden cigar box. The box was full of pocket watches. He took them out one by one and showed them to me. He let me listen to them tick and opened the back of one so I could see the parts moving inside. I wanted one, but none was offered.

Magic of a Sort

When you are a child, everything is inexplicable, or slightly magical—or so ordinary as to pose no questions. In my own time, if a question was asked, the answer was either an outright lie, utter bullshit, or some other evasion, like "You're too young to know" or "Shhhhh, I'll tell you when we get home."

Mom almost always had a busy day ahead. There were morning chores: she tended her chickens, putting out their feed, gathering the eggs. Baking, churning butter, doing laundry on Wednesdays, sewing to be done. But once in a while she would linger in bed to enjoy being with us. It was quiet in the world, aside from the chatter of morning birds, a rare distant moo from the dairy barn, or a truck on its way to town. This is before I was old enough to attend school, before we had an indoor bathroom.

Our neighbor Peally lived about a quarter of a mile down the highway to the east, toward town. Peally had been Dad's friend from when Dad was a child. His name was Felix Jewell, but Dad couldn't say Felix: it came out Peally, as in "really." That became his name in our family. Peally had a field up the highway to the west with hay that he might have cut by hand with a scythe. He didn't have much in the way of modern machinery. But things were the way they were. So he might have gone to the field a day or two before to cut some of the hay, leaving it on the ground to dry, and return to load it onto his wagon and take it to his barn.

On this particular morning, Peally was returning early from the field, and we listened to the clip-clop of his horses' hooves on the pavement and the sound of the wagon's iron tires. It was a rhythmic, almost musical sound, which gathered prominence as it approached and achieved a naked clarity at its closest and then receded into the east toward Peally's farm.

As we grew older, we would run out to the highway when Peally was passing with a load of hay, and he would halt his mares so we could climb to the top of the load and ride home with him. It wasn't a long ride at all, just right. And then Peally would turn into his driveway and stop his horses under the huge mulberry tree so we could eat the ripe berries and look at the oriole nest a mere fifteen feet away as the bright orange parents came and went, feeding their chirping babies. The orioles seemed almost too beautiful to be real, something that could never be touched, and absolutely too fine to be in our own trees.

Jim and I roamed where we wanted to, down to visit Peally, or west to visit Margaret Logan and have a chat with Lee. Almost everybody had a few cats, but the Logans had thirty-two, on average, at any one time. For sure they didn't have any rats or mice. The cats came and went as they desired. Arriving from down the road or delivered by birth. Often with crossed eyes or extra toes from excessive inbreeding. Of course, they would leave on the highway, too, just go away or get run over, like my own cat, Elizabeth. I cried when a neighbor reported that he had seen a calico cat on the side of the road.

Magic of a Sort

When I was six years old, I stood one afternoon in Peally's living room speaking with Gladys Kruger, his housekeeper and full-time companion. She would chat with me as if interested in my every thought, as though I was a real person and not merely a child. Looking out Peally's living room window, I could see our cornfield across the highway and the border of trees where the short-line railroad had crossed our farm. I speculated for a few moments about what I might do when I grew up. Maybe she had asked. I must have included farmer in my list, which also included musician and magician. Nothing practical. I was already pretty sure that I did not want to be a farmer. And for some reason, I didn't believe that I could be either a magician or a musician. That left me with nothing to do but enjoy the moment. Continue being a child as long as I could. Play and pretend. That's pretty much what I have done all my life.

Dad's Mind

I see Dad sitting in his living room chair looking out the window. Not looking at anything in particular, his eyes not moving or following anything. Just gazing into some distant moment, without any expression or movement to tie him to the present.

He would occasionally say something like, "Give me a fulcrum, a place to stand, and a long enough lever, and I can move the world." Or, "If you've studied Latin, you can figure out the meaning of most any word." Or, "I'm not interested in raising sheep, because the damned ewes always give birth on the coldest nights of the year." Or, "A man once said to me that if you go through all thirty-two degrees of Masonry, it's the equivalent of a year of college English."

One spring afternoon we went to the home of Professor Thorp. Prof had been the superintendent and Latin teacher when Dad graduated from high school in 1928. Dad revered the man, who, in his retirement, ran a hatchery on his farm south of town on US Highway 36. We were greeted warmly.

"Good to see you, Edward. Sarah," he said to Dad and Mom. "And my, look at these sturdy boys. When are you going to put them to work?"

"Oh, any day now," Dad replied. Prof's daughter, Emily, was there, too.

"Sarah, you know Emily, don't you?"

"Yes, indeed," said Mom. Emily had long reddish hair that draped below her shoulders. She wore a green sweater that she had knitted for herself. We were there to get baby chicks, but every encounter had a social aspect; there was time for some conversation. Always about the weather.

Prof had coached the basketball team to a regional championship.

"That was an amazing team," he said. "You played some fine basketball, Edward. That last game of the tournament, you just couldn't seem to miss a shot. You and George Carstarphen. Some great players that year."

They talked like that. Laughing and naming all the team members. Emily seemed unusual, not quite comfortable with herself, yet very pretty.

It was the end of winter, late afternoon, with long shadows and golden light. We came away with three boxes of peeping yellow chicks, three hundred of them in the trunk of the blue Dodge. Made the car smell like warm baby chicks. Prof's unmarried daughter was the subject of Dad's conversation with Mom as we drove away. I must have been five years old, trying to make sense of what I had seen and what was being said. It seems there was something wrong with Emily, like she wasn't quite right. But it wasn't spelled out. It was being said in code to keep me out of the knowing. Whatever was wrong with her, Dad was sure he knew what she needed.

Walking to School One Morning

Walking to school one morning, I speculate on the conse-
quences of stepping on the cracks in the sidewalk. This
seems like an unfinished thought. Would it break my
mother's back? It was hard to make sense of the world you
lived in, and books didn't help.

You can always sharpen your pencil without permission.
Any other mission requires Miss Christine's blessing. She
sits behind a large oak desk at the back of the room, a rect-
angular beige cavern with twelve-foot ceilings. The hand-
cranked pencil sharpener juts out of the south wall next to
one of the large windows. I like a sharp, fine point and use
the machine frequently. When we write, the part that I like
best is crossing t's and dotting the i's. But it's fun to put the
cross on an f, too. Making s's is also fun. But I don't like
making A or B or Y. So when I have to write a bunch of
words, there is a good part and a bad part. The real bad part
is that I'm slow and everybody else is fast. Martha Tobin
can read good. She gets to color in a coloring book all the
time 'cause she finishes first. Or she gets to do an errand for
Miss Christine.

I enjoyed making the swastika arm on the number four
and putting the hat on the number five. Everything else
felt like work, but crossing and dotting was like dessert. In
general, schoolwork had the same appeal as eating Brussels
sprouts. It could be done, but only under duress. We had
little plastic scissors in bright colors. I could never make

16

the scissors work. I was left-handed. The problem wasn't obvious to me.

Reading was the most difficult of all. The process was full of pain and embarrassment. For reading, the first graders would be seated in a circle of little chairs at the front of the room. We would each be called on to read. I could only read slowly, each word bracketed by silence, each word suspended, frozen. No punctuation, no inflection. I looked at the pictures, wondering where Dick and Jane lived. I didn't know anyone named Sally. No one I knew had a dog named Spot. Maybe a cow, but not a dog. Most dogs were hunting dogs: bird dogs, coonhounds, foxhounds. Not fluffy spaniels. And there were no policemen in my town. I kept looking in my schoolbooks for the world I lived in. And I couldn't find it. People in the pictures did not live on farms. They didn't have cows and pigs.

My second-grade reader was new, bright red, crisp, and fragrant. I left it in the schoolyard overnight. It got rain soaked. The back thickened, the pages rumpled. There was a story about a pony. There was a mythical aspect to the story involving sleep. I didn't like it. Because I had a pony, it didn't seem important, and I didn't find the story about the Slow Pony interesting. My biggest pony, Mary, was willful and treacherous, taking every possible opportunity to sweep me from her back under low-hanging limbs or the clothesline. One day she kicked me in the forehead. The kick in the head was really my fault. I came too close and tried to grab her tail, and she kicked me real hard. I knew right after that it was the wrong thing to do but not before. A child's mind works that way. That happened in the afternoon. Mom called the doctor, and he made a house call. Mom held me down on the kitchen table while the doctor closed the wound with four metal clamps pressed one at a time into my forehead and closed with pliers. It hurt. I cried a lot. It left a broad, prominent scar.

There were other things in the books that bothered me. In my third-grade reader, boys wore knickers, calf-length pants gathered tightly in a cuff above long socks and high-top shoes. I wondered when boys had dressed that way.

There were books on the shelves that interested me. Airplanes on an aircraft carrier. But they were biplanes, clearly out of date. The war was over, and it had not been fought with biplanes. The books were never about the world I lived in.

Directly across the street from the school was a black-smith shop. Throughout the day the blacksmith's hammer could be heard clanging hot iron on the anvil. From the Farm Bureau a block away could be heard the moan and whine of the grain mill. In winter the radiators clicked and groaned as the metal expanded and contracted. The class-rooms were either too hot or too cold, never just right.

In the basement under the school, Roy Miller, the janitor, tended the furnace. Sometimes Roy's seemed to be the only friendly face. He always spoke and had a smile for me. Maybe he was the only happy person there. Dad told me to introduce myself and always call him Mr. Miller. Later Mr. Miller insisted I call him Roy, because everyone did.

In the year I was in the first grade, all twelve grades were in one building. The dirt basketball court outdoors was flanked on one side by a wooden bleacher. In those years I

went barefooted whenever possible. The game must have
taken place in warm weather, because I was barefooted. It
occurred to me that if I went under the bleacher, I might
be able to see up women's dresses and learn something. I
looked up. The darkness and the angle of vision afforded me
no insight. With my attention focused above, I stepped on a
broken soda bottle, making a big cut on the left instep. Fred
Gould bathed it in peroxide and wrapped it with gauze. My
tetanus shot from after the horse kick was still good.

In the second grade, the concept of verbs and nouns,
adverbs, articles, and prepositions was presented in a work-
book called *Keys to Language*. But I didn't get it. I seemed
to speak pretty well without knowing the rules. So I must
have known the rules, at least in some sense. But that was
no comfort. I never completed assignments and had to stay
in without recess. Somewhere along the way, I speculated
that this was all preparation for adult life, making a living. It
was difficult to like school. It was just something you had to
do. I noted one day that when people said, "How are you?"
they expected to hear, "Fine." I began giving more complex
and nuanced answers, but never optimistic or exuberant.

In the third grade, I discovered the *World Book Encyclopedia* and read it whenever I could. There it was: the
television image was scanned one line at a time, volcanoes
came from deep in the earth, atomic energy radiation could
be stopped by a certain amount of earth and lead, pyramids
were ancient and mysterious, pythons could be huge, the
Grand Coulee was pretty big.

In the forth grade, we read briefly from a book with careful line drawings of men with longbows dressed in funny

clothing. Now in my memory, it looked vaguely Celtic. I could never articulate the question, but I wondered, where the heck were these people? It looked tribal and clannish at a time in my life when only Indians had tribes, and it made no sense. It was definitely another time, but when? Nor did the story interest me.

When I was in the fifth grade, the English book had a sentence, a declarative statement, mentioning the *Saturday Review*. I wondered, is there really a magazine called the *Saturday Review*? Or was this simply a fictional sentence to illustrate a concept? I asked the teacher, Mrs. Lange, whose husband, Art, was a barber who had become cracked and was in the state mental institution. She didn't know. In college I was able to find the *Saturday Review*. But in college, when a classmate read an essay referring to Winnie the Pooh, I asked whether it was a fictitious story to illustrate a concept or was there really a story called "Winnie the Pooh."

I spent a lot of time in school daydreaming. Staring out the window. Crossing my eyes, closing one eye, then the other, to compare the disparity of the two points of view. I chewed on my pencils, notching the full length with teeth marks. I bit off the erasers. I carved on my desktop. I chewed paper into tiny spitballs and blasted them out through tubes of rolled paper. I made paper airplanes. I drew tiny images of battle scenes inspired by war stories and comic books. I depicted tanks exploding, airplanes firing rockets, streams of tracer bullets from machine guns. These things interested me.

This was my world.

4-H and Other Clubs

It was a morning in the first grade when Miss Christine told the class that Ronnie Sting had an announcement. Ronnie was the smallest kid in school, even smaller than me. Ronnie rose from his desk and walked to the front of the room. He turned and spoke.

"Next Saturday morning at ten-thirty me and Joe Griffin and my brother and Freddie are going to perform a trapeze act. Tickets will be five cents and the money will go to the March of Dimes." That really impressed me. What imagination! What daring! They were going to perform in front of a crowd. I could picture the whole thing. Sparkling costumes. Music. They were starting their own circus! I was filled with envy and expectation. That was Monday. Then on Wednesday, Ronnie made another announcement: they had decided they needed more practice, it would be put off to a later date. It was never mentioned again. That was the first grade.

I always wanted to do something that would win approval. I wanted to be popular, well-liked, good-looking. I envied the kids who played ball well, who had curly hair, who were taller, stronger, faster. When there were class elections, I wanted to be class president. I was never even nominated. I was a leader only in my daydreams.

As I sat at my desk gazing with a vacant stare out the window, my imagination roamed. I often fought off attacks on the school by armed Chinese Communists. Saving the day by throwing grenades, leading my fellow students in a counterattack. Or appearing in a circus act performing on a high wire. People who knew me far below gasping in awe.

My deepest longing was just to fit in and be accepted. Be liked and treated well. I always felt like an outcast. As if nobody liked me at all. I always felt that older kids picked on me. It felt like I was almost always chosen last for baseball games at recess.

I wanted to be a Boy Scout. I so admired the Scout uniform. The badges, the belts, the canteen. Just like being in the army. Camping, carving, starting a campfire. It just seemed exciting. But there was no Boy Scout troop in New London. So it wasn't possible.

Then, when I was in the third grade, I heard that there was going to be a 4-H Club starting at the Rocky Point School, the white country school south of town on Highway 36. The school was closed, but the building was still used for community meetings. The night of the first meeting, I arranged to go home with Kate Ling, who lived across from school. Kate was two grades ahead of me. And her dad and my dad were good friends. The two had graduated high school together. There was one difference. Kate's older sisters had gone to Europe after graduating from high school. They had bicycled from France to Italy and had had an audience with the Pope. The Lings were Catholics. It was just one of those small categories into which people were placed that rang some kind of bell. It said different, in some not easily definable way. Like there were differences between boys and girls.

It was already something to be going home with a girl—even though I wasn't spending the night. Just having supper and going to the meeting. I sat with her on the bus ride to her house. It was nice sitting next to a girl, even if she was Catholic.

When we got to her house, it was already getting dark, and she had to milk the cow. I went out to the barn with her and listened to the milk zipping squirt by squirt into the bucket as the cow munched down ground corn. Inside her home there were two marvels that set the home apart. Not the crucifix on the wall, but two unique doorstops. One was a coconut still inside its outer husk, a crude, heavy thing, exotic and deeply strange. The other was a section of petrified tree trunk millions of years old. How could one actually have these things?

After supper we walked across the highway to the one-room schoolhouse. The county agricultural extension agent was there. He explained that 4-H meant head, heart, hands, and health. I made no judgments about that list. It seemed to be as good a list as any. There were a bunch of different things you could do. Every member was to have a project. You could grow tomatoes. Make an apron or a dress. You could raise a pig or a sheep. You could plant a field crop. There were dozens of choices. I decided I would raise a baby beef. That seemed to be a project of some importance. Mom picked me up at the end of the meeting and I told her about my choice: baby beef. She said we didn't have any beef calves for me to raise as my project, so that would be a problem. The next day I told Dad I was going to raise a baby beef as my 4-H project. He said we didn't have any suitable beef calves and we weren't getting any. So that was a year with nothing to show for my interest.

At the end of the summer I went to the 4-H fair in Center, Missouri, just ten miles west of New London. I went out with twenty other 4-H-ers to judge cattle. I thought maybe I would get lucky. We went in a bus to a nearby farm. There were five steers in a pen. A man who knew cows talked about the qualities we looked for in a beef animal. Deep and broad behind the front legs. Flat back. And so forth. There were about twenty factors to consider. We were each given a card and a pencil and asked to evaluate the five animals and grade them. I did not do well in this contest. It was a big disappointment. I didn't complete a project, so I got no credit for the year.

The next year a 4-H Club was formed closer to home. The first meeting took place at the Higgenbottom house a half-mile down the road toward town. I went to the meeting with Mom and my brother Jim. The evening began with a discussion of what to call the new chapter. I suggested "The Better Future 4-H Club," which every-body thought a good name. I chose woodworking as my project, which was a good choice, because Gilbert Higgenbottom was a carpenter and he was leading the woodworking projects. Gilbert had worked as a set builder in Hollywood.

"Did you see 'Back to Bataan?' You know that ship that sank with all the smoke pouring from it during the landing? I built that ship. It was nothing but a big flat wall of three-eighths-inch plywood on a wood frame."

I didn't see how that could be true. But he said it was for sure. He helped me build a sawhorse, and it was a very good sawhorse. I don't think anybody remembered that

I had been the one with a good name for the club. And
nobody was interested in my sawhorse.

At the next 4-H fair, I gave a demonstration on how
to make a carnation corsage. I had gone with a group of
women to see the garden of a local flower grower and then
to the shop of a florist, where I watched a corsage being
assembled. I had obtained the various wires, ribbons, and
some carnations the day before the fair. I only had enough
carnations for one rehearsal. Good thing it was pretty
simple to do.

The demonstrations took place in a classroom in a room
with a couple of dozen people watching. The person before
me demonstrated the making of a rope halter, a very useful
thing on a farm. I was nervous as I began. I had three red
carnations, some white ribbon, several pieces of wire, a pair
of scissors, and a small pair of wire nippers. I cut the stems
from the carnations.

"This is called chenille wire," I said, holding what
looked like a green pipe cleaner. After a few careful
motions the corsage was joined, the green pipe cleaner
end wrapped around a pencil to make a nice curl, and all
was tied with a white ribbon bow. Somehow I managed to
describe each step as I made the corsage. Then I held the
finished corsage for all to see. The judge was delighted.
Said she never did have a notion how that was done. And
gave me a blue ribbon. I didn't feel triumph, just relief
that it was over. And a little silly: a farm boy making a
corsage—in public. It just felt odd. But there was Mom
sitting in the second row with a smile from ear to ear. She
was proud as a peacock. That counted for something.

Margaret Murphy's Leg

There were two Black women who helped Mom once in
a while, Finn Peoples and Margaret Murphy. Finn would
help with the ironing and laundry if Mom was sick, which
wasn't often. Dad worked at the post office, so he had to
have a pressed white shirt every day. It seems everything
had to be ironed in those days. Mom finally got a mangle
iron for ironing pillowcases and sheets. The big flat things.

Finn and Mom always had conversations. That's how
Mom learned about the Glascock family. Black people
always knew the stuff white people either didn't know or
couldn't tell you. But Mom was always respectful of the
ladies who helped and shared a lunch at her table. But that
didn't mean they would be invited for supper.

Except Margaret Murphy stayed overnight to be with us
when Mom and Dad went to Kansas City. Margaret cooked
supper and ate with Jim and me. It seemed odd to have
Mom away. She was almost always there with us except
when she went to the hospital. I was five years old at the
time, just after the war. It had been an overcast couple
of days. It didn't rain but kept looking like it might. The
weather fitted my mood. I didn't feel that warm toward
Margaret.

At bedtime Jim and I were in the double bed in the back
bedroom, our room. Jim must have been tired, because
he went to sleep right away. But I was watching Margaret
get ready for bed, because I knew she had a wooden leg. I
didn't know anybody else with a wooden leg, so this was

something special. I watched as she unstrapped the brown
leg and put it on the floor beside the bed.

"What happened to your leg?" I asked.

"Oh, I got hurt in a car accident, and they had to cut my
leg off. They couldn't fix it. I was eighteen years old. That
was a few years back before you was born."

"Did it hurt?"

"Heck yes it hurt. Ain't ever had nothing hurt like that.
I'm lucky I lived to tell about it." She got into bed next to
me. "Scoot over a bit, honey," she said. I moved over closer
to Jim.

"Where did you get your leg?"

"Well, first off I got home from the hospital and was feeling pretty low. What was I gonna do without no leg? For
sure I was gonna have to use crutches or a pair of canes.
Well, the preacher at my church went into the woods and
picked out a tree of just the right size and cut it down. And
he carved me a leg. He was a good man. It was a pretty
good leg, and I learned to walk with it. I wore that homemade leg for about twelve years. I got around just fine. Way
better than being on crutches. But it wasn't all I thought it
should be.

"One afternoon I got inspired with an idea. I sat down
at the kitchen table and wrote a letter to President Roosevelt. I told him about the accident and how I had this
leg made by my preacher. And I said, 'Mr. President, can
you get me a new leg? I would make my life so good.' It
was about two months before a letter came to me from the
president. He told me to go to a hospital over in Kansas
City, over where your mom and dad has gone just this

morning. The letter told me the person to ask for, and it said there would be a new leg waiting for me. And so I went there and saw that man. A doctor looked at me and they got me just the right leg.

"When they put it on me I could walk right away. They thought they was gonna have to train me. But they didn't have to. Every morning when I put this on, I thank the Lord and President Roosevelt. Now you go to sleep." And she turned off the light.

The next morning when I woke up, Margaret was already in the kitchen. Jim and I got dressed. It was summer, and we just wore short pants. We didn't wear shirts and we didn't wear shoes. The box of Wheaties was on the table and the pitcher of cream and the bowl of sugar. As I ate I looked at the ballplayer on the box of Wheaties. It was looking like rain again.

After breakfast Jim and I went into the smokehouse just behind our house. The smokehouse had hams hanging from the ceiling on wires so the rats couldn't get to them. There was a large wooden icebox with two doors, one side for the block of ice and one side for the things you wanted to keep cold. There were a couple of old chests with drawers full of books and things. If you opened the drawer, you would find that mice had eaten parts of some of the books. There were tools, wire, a pair of posthole diggers, buckets, plowshares, buckets, and part of a corn planter.

Jim and I were looking around for something to play with. We had toys and a Radio Flyer wagon. There was a sled hanging up in the ceiling, but we couldn't reach it, and there was no snow because winter was over. So we opened the lid of the corn planter seed bin and jiggled things. I picked up a part that was on the floor and held it in my hands. As I turned it, a loose bolt fell from it and landed on my toe. My toe began to swell and turn blue. I went crying to Margaret.

"Well, there ain't nothing to be done. Just leave it be and in a little while you'll be fine."

It was two more days before Mom and Dad got back. That seemed like a long time. They had never been away for so long. My toe had turned black and was still swollen. It got worse and had to be lanced. The nail never quite grew back. It made me like Granddad, with his split big toenail. It was no comfort to have a toe like him.

I forgot the pain, and life went on. Margaret would still come to help out now and then. Her wooden leg was hollow and had a hole in the side so it could breathe.

One Day, Maybe More

I'm gettin' up and I don't feel like it. Not much. Don't
know why. Be happier if I could just stay in bed or if it
was Saturday. Then I wouldn't have to go to school. I like
recess OK, but not school.

This here is my bed that Mom and Dad bought for me
and my brother Jim at St. Louis from Uncle Dick Slack's
furniture store. Mom says it's a big store and real famous
because they have a radio program each morning on
KMOX. Cowboy music just like Gene Autry plays. Bed's
made out of maple, and you can see by the covered wagon
on the headboard that it's special. Mom says the name of
the bed is "Prairie Schooner." It's real important to Mom.

For breakfast I'm having cereal with sugar and cream.
Mom skims the cream from the milk that we get from the
dairy barn. I walk over there and carry a whole gallon back
every night. We get so much cream we give it to the cats. I
like cream on my cereal and I like sugar, about three or four
spoonfuls. Kellogg's Corn Flakes is my favorite. But I have
Wheaties sometimes. It's the breakfast of champions. And
I like Rice Krispies because the three elves on the box are
named Snap, Crackle, and Pop. The cereal is supposed to
talk, but I can't hear it say anything. I like shredded wheat
because of the nice picture of Niagara Falls on the box.
We pretend the shredded wheat is a little bale of hay. I like
looking at the package while I'm eating breakfast because
there's nothing else to look at except my brother Jim, and I
look at him all the time. Except not so much now that I'm

in school and he doesn't get to go for another year. I'm in the first grade.

Jim doesn't say much. When he talks, nobody can understand him but me. When he says "Bowbie" and "Ree-a-rah" he means money. We don't have any except when we go to town on Saturday. Then we get a nickel to buy a comic book. I like Donald Duck best. Some people think Jim and me look just alike. But I don't know 'cause I can't see myself.

When Mom buys chicken feed, she looks at all the bags to decide which one looks the best. She calls it a cotton print. So I wear cotton print shirts made by my mom.

Mom wants me to finish my breakfast so I won't miss the school bus. "Hurry up," she says, "it will be here any minute." She sounds mad. I don't know why. I never know why Mom and Dad are mad. Dad says children are to be seen and not heard, so when he's mad, I better not say anything or, well, I might get slapped. That means I'm not supposed to ask questions, so mostly I don't.

I'm supposed to wait out next to the highway for the bus except when it's cold or raining. Then I wait inside next to the front door. There used to be a fence around the front yard. One day I cut my foot on a broken bowl out by the back porch. I was barefoot 'cause my brother and me, we don't wear shoes in the summer. But I wear shoes to school and I take 'em off when I get home. Except if it's cold.

Here comes the bus now. Orville Lucas is the bus driver, and it's his bus. Orange and black. It's a Ford. But it ain't a real school bus. It's a panel truck for delivering potato chips or something like that. Inside we sit on two wooden benches. I like to sit next to the big boys. But sometimes they pinch me. If I sit next to a girl, somebody will say I'm in love with her. I hate that. Except for Janie Lou, 'cause she's pretty as a picture and has long curly brown hair. Her big brother Lyle Wayne has curly hair, too. It's dark and curly. He combs it back real nice, and it has a nice bunch of curls on top of his forehead.

Stuart thinks I'm ugly. I know 'cause he said to me, "You ugly little son of a bitch, I'd like to cut your nuts out." Stuart is Tom Lake's brother and he works on the farm. Sometimes he carries a black snake whip. If he's got to move the bull, he has that whip in his hand. Or else he's got a shotgun. Mom says he's a coward. She said if she had to move the bull, all she'd need is a stick of wood. I told Mom what Stuart said to me and she told him, "Stuart, I will not put up with that kind of talk to my children." I think she should have smacked him.

One time I called Dad a son of a bitch. Dad was sitting at the supper table, and I said to him, "You son of a bitch." It made him mad and he took his belt off and whipped me. It hurt something awful, and I cried real hard.

That time when Stuart said those bad things to me, I was in the barn with Jim. We was in the hayloft watching Stuart and Bill Brown cut some baby pigs. It was real scary 'cause them pigs squeal really loud when you cut 'em. That means to take them pigs' nuts out. Most of the time they wait until the pig is more growed up, and then you can eat those nuts. Mom cooks 'em and they're pretty good eatin' if you don't know what they are. And you wouldn't know 'cause they call 'em Rocky Mountain oysters.

I like to be in the hayloft. We can play up there and jump in the hay. When it rains, the tin roof makes a good sound, and one time my brother Jim and me, we just laid down in the hay and went to sleep.

When the school bus comes I say to Orville, "Good morning, Mr. Lucas." You have to say Mr. or Mrs. to anybody who is grown up, unless they are your relative. I call Cousin Virge "Cousin Virge." But if a grownup is Black, then sometimes you call them Uncle or Aunt, even though they are just people you know. Aunt Mandie is a Black lady who lives down the road. Mom says Aunt Mandie was a slave and she's at least a hundred years old. And Uncle Dan Mason is real old, too. He lives down on Uncle Rec's farm and he's real poor. He goes to town in a wagon that's all held together with baling wire.

But there's some Black people I can call by their name. Like Basil Stuart, who comes out sometimes to clean out the hen house. I can sit in his lap and he reads to me. Then there's James Otis, who's Black, and I call him James Otis. He works for Uncle Charles Lemon, who is not Black and is not my uncle. But Dad said I should call him Uncle Charles anyway. And if somebody is a preacher, you call him Reverend. And you call the teacher Miss Christine or Miss Fanny even if she's married. Which Miss Fanny is and Miss Christine is, too.

Miss Christine teaches first grade and second grade and third grade. She says she has eyes in the back of her head and can see what we're doing even when she seems to be looking the other way. If you're bad, she makes you stand in the corner.

My favorite part of school is recess, and the part I hate most is reading. We have to sit in chairs in a circle for reading. I read real slow, and it makes me want to cry. I wish I had a radio inside my shirt so that Mom could read for me. But I don't have no radio like that.

On Christmas, I got to go run an errand for the teacher. Charlie Rule and me walked to Miss Christine's house to get her Christmas gifts for the pupils. It was bags of candy and nuts, and she had them in a washtub. Me and Charlie had to carry this tub all the way from her house to the school. There was snow everywhere, and it was cold and my nose was running. And I didn't have no gloves. When we got back, there was noise and steam coming out of the radiators. And me and Charlie stood next to the radiator to get warm.

When we have music, Miss Christine plays the piano and we sing. "The Red River Valley" is my favorite. It is sad, but I like the way it sounds. "Come and sit by my side if you love me." That part is nice, but then comes the sad part. "For they say you are leaving this valley, and the one who has loved you so true." That's real sad, isn't it?

Sometimes we play with sticks and sandpaper blocks. Some kids get to play triangles or the cymbals. I want to play the cymbals, but I never get to. I always have to play the sandpaper blocks. That's no fun at all.

Mom Never Puts on Airs

Mom never cared much for dressing up or putting on airs—well, mostly not. She did wear a hat with a veil to church on Sundays in the years when women did that. And there was the time when she was in the Eastern Star and all the ladies wore gowns for the ceremonies. Mom held the station of Ruth and wore a yellow gown and learned the words to be said for her part. She seemed to like it for a while and then seemed to lose interest.

She did think it was important to look nice. She would wear a nice dress to the Laugh-a-Lot Club, which met in various homes on the first Wednesday of each month, with a carry-in dinner at noon. A meeting followed the meal, and there was a reading or a demonstration in the meeting. They were always learning some kind of craft, and Mom was always doing some kind of project. She enjoyed making things and took pride in what she did.

When I was in the first grade, I wanted the cowboy outfit in the Sears catalog—the one with the picture of a rearing horse on each side of the chaps. And a vest with fringes. Instead, I got a vest and chaps made by Mom. She was so proud that she had stencil-painted a cactus on each leg. And put rickrack decoration on the vest. To me, they just looked homemade. Every kid knew that store-bought was better.

Mom made all my clothes until I was in school. And she made all my shirts, except for the white dress-up ones, until I was in the fifth grade. She even made little dresses for my friend Sharon Anne Niday and charged a dollar and a half for each one. I played in the yard with Sharon after she tried on the new dresses. Her mom worked with my dad at the post office.

One thing that was clear to me about clothes was that blue jeans were better than overalls. Overalls had a bib, and I hated them because at school, all the older boys wore blue jeans with a belt at the waist. Only little kids and old men wore bib overalls. I wanted to be like the older boys, not like the farmers.

One afternoon when I got off the school bus, I was greeted by my younger brother, Jim, wearing a new pair of jeans. I was overcome by jealousy and ran crying to the house. How could he wear this symbol of grownup-ness while I wore overalls with shoulder straps? I was dressed like a little boy while my little brother dressed like someone much older. Gerry Lake, who lived in the little white house across the road, had decided that she liked Jim and had bought the pants for him as a gift. He was real proud, while I was just miserable. How come she didn't get any for me? What was wrong with me? I felt that I had no importance at all. I cried and cried because Gerry didn't get jeans for me. I guess Gerry liked Jim better than she liked me.

In second grade, all the girls wore dresses, except Donna Stringer. Donna wore boy's jeans that buttoned up the front, not on the side, like girls' pants were supposed to. I had a crush on Donna. She had brown eyes and long black hair with curls. Even though she wore jeans, I didn't hold that against her. We wrestled one day at lunchtime on the play-ground. I liked the fact that we touched. But she pretty much beat me up, sat on top of me and pinned me to the ground. It wasn't a real fight or anything like that, and nobody paid any attention. I had started it. I liked her, but she didn't like me. That was pretty much the end of that romance.

There were a couple of girls who seemed to like me. In the first grade, it was Kay Lynn Record. Her dad worked at the REA, the Rural Electric Co-Op. And in the third grade, Becky Shelburne was my girlfriend. Becky was silly, could laugh about almost anything, and the teacher called her Goofball. Becky lived with her grandmother, Mrs. Hoffmeyer, a smart and funny woman who was secretary of the draft board. Many years later she showed me a touch of generosity, perhaps owing to my brief special relationship with Becky, by stamping my draft card to extend my draft liability to age thirty-five.

Zoe Hayden had always been a friend, a better-than-average friend, and we shared a birthday. She was pretty with blond hair. But we were strictly just friends.

I often talked with Mom while she ironed or sewed or churned butter. We would take turns cranking the churn. She had views on a wide range of subjects. She read the newspaper and would tell me of something she had noticed. She loved Eleanor Roosevelt, thought of her as a woman of courage and principle, admiring the fact that Mrs. Roosevelt arranged for Marion Anderson to sing at the Lincoln Memorial when the Daughters of the American Revolution wouldn't rent their hall to a Black singer.

Poor people were of a different class and didn't get invited to your house for dinner. That was why Mom's

family didn't often come to celebrate Christmas or any
other gathering when Dad's parents were invited. It was
never explained. I just understood, and it made me feel odd.
There were rules for the way people behaved with each
other. But I didn't know the real why of them.

There were people in the community who seemed
important, like the banker. And there was John S. Wood,
who owned the farm that joined Dad's land on the south.
John S. Wood was a St. Louis banker, a man who owned
land in the country but lived in the city. During the war,
John S. Wood was on a national control board of some kind
having to do with rations. When one of Dad's hired hands
destroyed a tractor tire and there were none to be had in
the stores, Dad called long distance to speak with John S.
Wood about the need for a tractor tire. And Dad was able to
buy one. Dad was proud of this special relationship with a
powerful man. Mom would never mention a thing like that.

There was always a huge gap between my parents. More
than just between man and woman. Mom was curious.
She read things. She made things. She loved museums
and exhibits. Historic places. Dad was never interested
in museums and read little other than the daily papers,
magazines, and Zane Gray's fiction. Whenever we went to
St Louis, Mom would go shopping in the morning and to
the zoo or the museum in the afternoon. My brothers and
I would go with her. Dad would go to the St. Moritz Bar
and Grill, owned by his friend Felix Motini, a Swiss-Italian
immigrant who would come to hunt quail with Dad in the
fall. Dad would spend the entire day in the smoke-filled
bar drinking and talking. When he returned, he smelled

strongly of smoke and whiskey, and his mood turned dark. He could quickly lash out at me or my brothers. And he would argue with Mom. It made me miserable.

Going West

My mother, Sarah, is strong and tough-minded, with a certain creative bent of mind. A willingness to try new things, up to a point. An enthusiasm for any new art form promoted by *Woman's Home Companion* or demonstrated by the county agent's assistant at the most recent Women's Extension Club meeting. She sews, embroiders, quilts, and in the course of time has etched glasses and aluminum trays, painted the trays, and painted a bunch of plaster figurines. She has among her most personal private treasures a paper she wrote for a high school class that contains carefully wrought Egyptian hieroglyphs. One is the symbol for Ra, the Sun god. On another paper a set of delicate drawings depict the three styles of Greek columns, drawn and labeled in pencil: Doric, Ionic, and Corinthian. She appreciates these images without any desire to travel to Egypt or Greece. She is interested in any museum, whether it houses a log cabin or paintings by Rembrandt.

One day we take off on a family trip. Our ultimate destination is Yellowstone, and we arrive there midmorning on a hot summer day. My dad, Ed, tells the park ranger at the gate that we have no firearms, but I know there's a twelve-gauge shotgun in the trunk. After we leave the gate, I ask Dad about the gun.

"God dammit!" he snaps angrily. "If I'd a told him I had a gun, I'd have to leave it here. And we plan to leave by a different gate. And besides, it's none of your damned business." And that ends the conversation.

The motor of the Hudson drones as we drive through tall trees. At sunset we reach Yellowstone Falls. The valley is so beautiful it seems heavenly. Even Ed is impressed, but he has no words for it. We drive to a site much closer to the falls and the thunderous sound of descending water. I wonder if I am too close to the edge. Will I fall? Will the earth collapse under me? Will I fall through the air, descend with the water, crash into the river below?

The next morning, we visit Old Faithful. We go into the Old Faithful Inn, and it is here that I am truly filled with awe. The building is a giant log cabin. A marvel. And even the six-year-old child that I am feels the scale and wonder of the structure. I stand looking up at the balcony, knowing that it is all special, that it is the work of men, and that it is lovely, magical, and grand. Also that it is something from a past that is lost and just this small bit of grandeur remains. The beams, the banisters. Every detail made from the natural shape of a tree trunk or limb. And I try to imagine who made this so long ago and feel desperate sadness about the fragility of this past. That we may forget and nothing will remain.

Outside, we wait for Old Faithful to blow off. It is still early morning, and the air is cool.

A ranger makes a little speech about Old Faithful. The gathering is only a few dozen in number. Sarah is holding the baby. In the quiet, Ed makes small talk with people standing near us. They're from Keokuk, Iowa.

"I've been there several times," Ed says. "Drove twice and took the Burlington once." The man says he works for the Burlington.

"I worked a whole summer for the Burlington," Ed tells the man. "On the rip track in Hannibal, where they tear apart old boxcars. I jumped out of one of those boxcars onto a four-by-four with a spike nail. That nail came right out of the top of my shoe. Had to pry my foot off that spike with a crowbar. The old man I was working with took off the bandana he wore around his neck and tied a cud of chewing tobacco to the top and bottom of my foot. I tell you, it sure was something."

Wherever Ed goes, he tells little stories about his life in Missouri. It is a world he knows. It is a realm he understands. Wherever he goes, he will always come back to Missouri.

Class in a Small Town

Early in my childhood, I managed to get a sense that some people were better than others. That it was shameful to be poor, mentally retarded, divorced, an orphan, or adopted. Being a criminal, an ex-convict, a cheat, liar, two-timer, bastard, or Republican wasn't acceptable either. Or a cocksucker, whatever that was. Also, it wasn't so good to be a Baptist or a Holy Roller. Or a Catholic. Especially, for some reason, a Catholic. Johnny Briscoe said you called Catholics "mackerel snappers" because they ate fish on Fridays.

And clearest of all was the message that it was not a good thing to be a Black person because there were lots of names for them. I knew they had a bad lot, because they never got invited for dinner and never had important jobs. And they all seemed poor. Except for the ones who came back from Chicago in the bright yellow Packard. But even if they had a Packard and dressed better than anybody I ever knew, they were still Black people and would always be. Why else did they have their own toilets at the state fairgrounds, have to sit upstairs at the movies? And they had their own school over at the edge of town, which was just one room with one teacher.

The town's social organizational chart must have been quietly laid down for me. Probably a shrug here, a wink there, or a small change of tone in the voice. Mom could be severe with a squint of the eye, a smirk. It was never a lecture, seldom a direct condemnation. I had to work out my own scheme for evaluating the status of anyone new. Like when Bob German, son of the owner of the dry cleaners, Arlen German, came home from Germany with a German girl as his wife. I was certain that there was just something slightly dishonorable about it. The woman must have been an undesirable. Maybe Mom even said something. Once a new family moved into town so poor they dried the laundry by draping it over the fence. Mom spoke with compassion about their situation. She felt sorry for them. It was not so good to have people feel sorry for you. Except if somebody had cancer. Then it was OK.

It was as clear as the nose on your face that Mom's family was of a lower quality than Dad's. How could I know that was so? By watching who Dad's parents played cards with and the people they invited over for dinner. They would never invite Black people for dinner, or poor people, or Mom's folks. Mom's folks were never invited anywhere, except to visit their own relatives. But Grandmother Glascock and Aunt Lucy were in the DAR. They knew our ancestors all the way back to Bathsheba and which ancestor arrived on these shores in 1699. And they knew everybody in town. And if you weren't in the Daughters of the American Revolution, you probably weren't anybody.

Mom regarded the DAR as a pompous bunch who thought they were more important than everyone else. Mom had no kind words for them. They treated her like dirt whenever they could, taking every possible opportunity to slight her or cause misery by imposing on her. I didn't understand all of these things in my youngest years, and yet I always understood that there was a class difference.

When Mom's parents finally moved to New London,
they only knew the next-door neighbors and never did get
to know anybody else. They never went anywhere except
to shop for groceries or shoes. And they'd never traveled
farther than Hull, Illinois, and Kansas City. And that was to
visit relatives. Dad said of Mom's father, half in admiration,
half in disgust, "He never bought anything that he didn't
pay cash for, not a car, not a washing machine, not even
a house. He doesn't owe anybody a dime, never has. But,
on the other hand, he couldn't buy anything on credit if he
wanted to."

If you worked at the courthouse, you were probably
somebody. If you sat across the street on the bench in front
of McGowan's Paint and Wallpaper during the day drunk
on wine, you were nobody. But then, it was Basil Stuart
who did that, and he was Black, even when he was sober.
If you had lots of money, owned lots of land, or used your
middle initial in your name, you were somebody, like John
S. Wood, who was an attorney and helped Dad get the
tractor tire he needed during the war. So when I was in the
second grade, I decided to use my middle initial when I
put my name on my assignments, and to make myself even
more important, I added a flourish under the name. I don't
think it made any difference in my grades.

The other thing that was bad was to have somebody nuts
in your family. You could be "not quite right" in the head.
That was OK. There were plenty of people like that. But
if you had to be committed to the state insane asylum, that
was very bad, because it meant you were nuts. My sixth-
grade teacher's husband was a barber who repaired radios

when he wasn't giving a haircut. Well, Art got depressed and had to be put away. I would ask Mrs. Lange every once in a while how Art was doing. She would sheepishly say, "Oh, about the same." In my heart I knew my teacher's husband was nuts.

It was interesting to me that it was important to drive a nice car. We drove a Hudson. I didn't think it was a nice car. Maybe just because we owned it. Mrs. Croll drove a Lincoln. That seemed important, because she was important, because everyone thought she was rich. It was also important if you drove a Cadillac. I wanted us to drive one, but Dad wasn't interested. But even if you owned a Cadillac and were Black, people might envy you and look down on you at the same time.

Dad was on the board of the Ralls County State Bank for many years. It wasn't a job, it was a position. He had been one of the founders of the bank. Maybe he put some money into some shares or something. And Lillard was the banker. I always thought Lillard was somebody. Maybe because he was the banker and he was fat, I thought of him as somebody big. But Lillard had made some questionable loans. So Dad resigned from the board, saying that he was tired of getting his ass chewed out by the state bank examiners over Lillard's bad judgment.

The curious thing was figuring out who was somebody and who wasn't somebody, and in spite of the way Dad's family looked down on Mom's family, people in Dad's family still claimed their own wherever they stood in the community. Cousin Bert was an alcoholic painter and paper hanger, in essence a drunk, but he was still our cousin. At the other extreme, there was Cousin Henry, who owned the telephone company. From the way he dressed, you'd never think he owned anything. But Dad said the old man, Henry's father, had bought thousands of shares of AT&T when it was eighteen cents a share.

"Hard to know what your Cousin Henry's worth."

The Postcard

Throughout my childhood, we never saw Dad in the mornings because, as postmaster of a small town, he had to be at the post office at 5:30 each day. The day began with the rural carriers sorting the mail for their routes, placing it in the rack of slots rising from the back of their respective sorting tables. Dad, along with his clerk, sorted mail for the P.O. boxes facing into the lobby. These were rented to townspeople or anyone who wanted to get their mail at the post office. If you didn't want to pay quarterly rent, you could always ask for your mail at the front window. That was called General Delivery.

The lobby door was unlocked at 7:00 a.m.; the service window opened at 8:00 and stayed open till 5:00 p.m. After the mail was sorted and the rural carriers had left for their routes branching out from town along the highways and gravel farm-to-market roads, Dad would take a breakfast break for toast and coffee at Naylor's fountain a few doors down the street. He treasured this time, chatting with whoever was there. As postmaster he knew every man, woman, and child in town and six miles in all directions in the surrounding countryside—by name and street address.

Dad had actually wanted to be a rural carrier like his father, who for many years had delivered mail by horse and buggy. There were plenty of lean times in farm living: a dry year might mean poor crops, a wet springtime might mean crops would be planted too late, and in a year of bumper crops, overabundance would depress the market.

A government job meant there would be a check weekly, whatever happened with the weather or the markets. So Dad took the civil service examination and passed with a good score.

Dad tells how one evening in 1941 he went to meet with Judge Scott, the local arbiter of Democratic patronage, to see if he couldn't get assigned a rural route. He sat at the kitchen table with the judge and his seven-year-old son, talking about local matters in the way that one does. It just doesn't make sense in a small town to get to the point too soon. The judge served iced tea. If Dad had been older and more of a peer to the judge, he would have been offered whiskey.

"Eddie," he finally said to Dad, "I know you been wanting that rural mail carrier position, and you passed the civil service test just fine. But you know, Biggs Briscoe wants that job, and he's in line ahead of you, so I can't give you that. I'm real sorry, too."

There was a long silence as the disappointment settled in. Then his son broke the quiet.

"Daddy, Mr. Glascock could be postmaster, couldn't he?"

"Yeah, Eddie, I see no reason why you couldn't be postmaster. A couple of other people want that job, but they didn't pass the exam. So it's yours if you want it."

So Dad became postmaster in November 1942. Having this job, Dad offered himself many small luxuries, one of which was an annual trip to the national postmasters convention, wherever it might be. That always meant travel to distant places by train. The conventions were mostly occasions to meet fellow postmasters and drink with them.

Dad took it upon himself to get other postmasters to join the National Association of Postmasters and would drive from town to town in the northeastern part of the state enlisting them. One result was that Dad got to know a goodly portion of the state's postmasters on a first-name basis.

Dad would stand in line at any postal function to meet and shake hands with the assembled dignitaries. He enjoyed being with people, especially if they were having a drink. He counted Barney Dickman, the postmaster of St. Louis, among his friends. He counted the postal inspectors who came periodically to audit his office among his friends. He was comfortable with these people, and he always had a few drinks with them.

One of his proudest accomplishments had to do with a conversation on the train to one of the conventions. He was talking to someone in the lounge car, a businessman on his way to Philadelphia. The man knew markets, and they talked about things that affected commodities. And Dad knew a few things about that, shipping cows and grain, the ups and downs.

It somehow came around to the postmasters on the train. Dad was given to a bit of bragging when he'd had a drink. On this occasion Dad boasted that although he was only a second-class postmaster, he was actually pretty well known in Missouri. "If you address a three-cent postcard to 'Eddie, Missouri,' it'll get to me" was the bet. The conversation was forgotten and the convention greatly enjoyed.

A couple of months later, a card was forwarded to Dad from the dead letter office in St. Louis. It was simply addressed "Eddie, Mo."

The Postcard

"Eddie, if you get this I want to hear from you." "Bill Coleman, 1723 6th Street, Omaha, Nebraska" was jotted on the back. Dad sent a letter thanking him for the card. And bragged about it for the next forty years.

Rabbit on the Ceiling

Early one fall morning, Jim and I got into bed with Mom. That opportunity was rare because Mom was usually up when we woke. We talked about the rabbit on the ceiling. It was visible only at a certain time of the early morning, after Dad had gone to work. The rabbit was a crack in the ceiling plaster. We could clearly see the ears and front paws, the line of the back, the wiggly nose. It wasn't actually wiggling, but we knew it would.

Outside, the sun was coming up, and we could hear our neighbor Peally's horses clip-clopping on the concrete of Highway 19. As we listened, we looked at the ceiling above the bed and talked about the rabbit. What it might be doing, what it might have had for breakfast. It wouldn't have had a Nabisco shredded wheat biscuit with cream and sugar like we would. It wouldn't have had a glass of milk. It wouldn't have played in a sand pile. Would it eat some carrots in our garden? Well, it just might.

After we had eaten our breakfast, Jim and I would go out to the highway as Peally came back with his load of loose hay. He would stop and pull us up to the top, and we would ride with him down the highway. The sky was blue overhead without a single cloud.

Behind Peally's house, next to the barn lot gate, was a white garage where he kept his black 1939 Nash. On the wall was nailed every metal Missouri license plate he had ever bought, one for each year he had owned a car. We would go into the house, and Gladys, Peally's housekeeper, would give us each a glass of water. She would be listening to "As the World Turns" with its organ music and important-sounding announcer. Peally was an old man then. But most farmers kept on farming as long as they could, because that's what farmers did.

Jim and I walked back up the road on the grassy shoulder. There was only an occasional passing car or truck, and people didn't drive fast in those days. Even so, Mom would always warn us to be careful when crossing the highway. Every morning at 9:30, a blue and white bus went by on its way to Mexico, Missouri, about forty miles west and south. It came back in the afternoon. If you wanted to ride the bus, you just stood at the side of the road and it would stop for you. We only rode it once in a while, to Hannibal.

The highway must have been a little scary, because I often dreamed about it. In my dream I would be playing on the concrete with my toys. My blue metal truck, my plastic Farmall tractor with matching red wagon, the wooden blocks with brightly colored sides. I would hear the hum of an approaching truck and begin to remove my things from the road. I would move as quickly as I could, but my body was like lead. I seemed to be frozen, unable to run or walk, barely able to crawl as the truck came faster and faster, closer and closer. I never seemed to actually get out of the road.

The last time wheat was harvested using a threshing machine instead of a combine was 1945, when I was four years old. The big machine was placed in the field right behind the barn and not far from the silo and the bullpen. The wheat was cut in the field using a binder that tied the stalks with heads of grain into bundles, which were gathered and stacked as shocks to be thrown onto the horse-drawn wagons and hauled to the thresher. The thresher was a big box-like machine with many wooden parts that made a lot of noise and dust. The whole thing was powered with a long pulley belt running from the tractor some thirty feet away. On one end of the thresher, a big open mouth with grabbers pulled the bundles inside, where all kinds of things shook and roared, with straw blowing out of one long pipe on top and grain flowing into a bin.

It took lots of people to harvest this way: two men to operate the thresher, one man to drive each wagon and team of horses, of which there were several. Someone had to operate the horse-drawn binder in the field, a couple of men collected the bundles into shocks, and several more loaded the wagons. At noon, Mom would serve a big dinner for the whole crew. Fried chicken, mashed potatoes, sliced tomatoes, corn on the cob, and green beans with iced tea. For desert there would be pie.

When the threshing was done, there would be a pile of straw the size of a chicken house. The threshing crew would fold up the machine like a carnival ride, and the whole outfit would move on up the road to the next farm, where it would all be unfolded to start over. I rode along on a wagon as they left our farm that day, and Margaret Local called Mom to say, "Sarah, if you're missing a boy, I might just have him."

Rabbit on the Ceiling

Jim and I could go anyplace on the farm, but we knew
not to go into the bullpen. One afternoon at milking time,
we were playing on the huge stack of new straw behind
the big cow barn, not far from the bullpen, which ran
from the back of the barn a hundred and fifty feet to the
east and then to the north about halfway to the abandoned
railroad track. The bull was a Jersey, with forward-curled
horns and a shiny brown body that blackened gradually at
its stout shoulders. As Jim and I climbed up and slid down
the haystack time after time, the bull began to paw the
ground and kick dirt over its shoulder, all the while growl-
ing deeply and glaring at us. Finally Tim Lake, Dad's
partner at that time, came out from the barn and yelled at
us, "Get the goddamned hell out of there! You're making
the bull mad, you little bastards."

Chocolate Drop

It must have been because of my upbringing. Not really
having any contact with Black persons of my own age that
I have come to feel always slightly aware of them as Black
persons. When I was a child in rural America, there were
plenty of Black people around, and I even knew a few of
them: Finn Peoples, who used to come out and work for
my mother once in a while on housework. The same was
true for Margaret Murphy, who had a wooden leg. Now the
interesting thing is that my folks always spoke of these two
ladies with respect. But there might have been an under-
standing that they wouldn't have to pay them very much for
the work they did. But that was never mentioned.

Margaret Murphy sang a song while she worked: "Shoo
fly pie, apple pan dowdy, can't get enough of that wonderful stuff." That must have been around 1945 or '46.

And then there was Basil Stewart. Basil was a drunkard
and spent a lot of his time sitting on the courthouse lawn
or in front of McGowan's paint store on the corner, where
he could watch everybody go by. Sometimes if Basil was
particularly drunk, the sheriff would put him in jail until
he sobered up. Dad hired Basil for a couple of days each
year to clean out the chicken house. At noon he would wash
his hands and come into the house for dinner. Dinner was
the noon meal, and Basil ate it at the table with Mom and
Dad and us boys. But I thought it odd that when we had a
threshing crew for dinner with fifteen or twenty men, the
Blacks and children ate in the kitchen and all the white men

ate in the dining room. I just felt real strange about that. No one said anything about it. That was just the way it was.

Of course, I did live in a small rural town. And it is characteristic for small town people to feel strange about anybody who is different or from the outside. Not that the Blacks were from the outside, although they did live in a certain part of town, sort of across the tracks, as they say. Mom always talked to the ladies who worked for her, and as far as I could tell, it was a cordial relationship. But I was young, so a lot would have passed by me.

There were several Black people who lived on the Mason property, some eight or ten acres at the back of my uncle's farm. The land must have been ceded to the Mason family when slavery ended. Old Dan Mason drove a team of horses into town once a week to buy what provisions he needed. He must have been in his eighties. That was about 1947, give or take a couple of years. Mom said she had seen Old Dan trying to climb the fence one day, so she went to see what was the matter. Could she help? It was a positive relationship, as far as I could tell. His Social Security or pension check had blown over the fence as he'd gotten down off the wagon to close the gate. Mom found the fluttering paper and brought it back to him. The amount was two dollars. Dan seemed so very poor. Outside his three-room house was a large garden with corn, tomatoes, and lots of squashes. Potatoes and beets and greens, chickens, too. And a pig. It was a hard life for this old man.

Just down the road from us was Aunt Mandy, who had actually been a slave. Aunt Mandy's house was on a small tract at the east end of our farm, across the highway from

Carl Tisher's farm. Nobody seemed to know for sure how old she actually was. Dad was sure she was at least one hundred years old. That would mean that she was born in 1845. Dad said that whenever he was driving to town and she was walking to town, he would stop to give her a lift. He would have to insist that she get into his car. She didn't want to be beholden to nobody. He said, if she saw you coming, she might turn around and pretend she was walking in the other direction. She died in the fire when her house burned down. That must have been around 1945 or '46. I can remember her as a real person existing in the world, but I have no image of her. The house was one of two on that three-acre piece, both completely devoid of paint.

I never got to know any Black children. They were off in their own world at the edge of town. One day as I was playing in the schoolyard, and two Black children about my own age were walking on the other side of the street. They had been uptown and were on their way home. I yelled out to them, "Chocolate drops!" I don't think I said anything else. When I told my mother that I had done this, I was soundly reprimanded. It was made clear that I was to act respectfully toward the Blacks. The thing I remember after I called the Black children chocolate drops was that I didn't feel all that good about it.

After the Brown decision in 1954, the Black kids went to our school. It saved the school district a lot of money because it was able to eliminate one teacher, the Black one, and no longer had to pay tuition for all the Black kids to go to a much better high school in the adjacent larger city.

Most of the white kids got along fine with the Black kids. But the Black kids were still on the bottom of the local social structure. And that was that.

On the other hand, they had their own view of things, too. One of the Perkins kids yelled out to me as I walked past the lumber yard, where he worked for the summer, "Hey Baylis, you gonna wear shoes over at the university?"

Two People Named Dick

There were two people in town named Dick, and they both lived in the same house even though they weren't related. Dick Edding was the barber whose shop was opposite the post office and next door to German's Dry Cleaners.

I went with Granddad one Saturday morning to Dick Edding's barber shop. We rode to town in his blue Dodge two-door sedan, which seemed to have an extra-long trunk, because the passenger compartment was shorter than the ones on four-door sedans. This was a special day because I didn't get to go places with Granddad very often.

The barber shop had a candy cane sign out front with a spiral of red and white stripes and a white ball on top, just like it was supposed to. There was a mirror on the wall behind the barber chair and a towel steamer with a ball-shaped top that opened like a giant eyelid, revealing the hot white towels. On the north wall were two benches, like park benches: long wood slats on an iron frame with a scroll rolling over slightly at the top of the back and at the front of the seat. And there were some chairs. On the wall was a seed corn almanac calendar, and on the ceiling a black metal fan with wood blades.

Granddad was pretty much bald, but he had hair around the sides, and to trim that he depended on Dick Edding: no man worth his salt would have his wife cut his hair, unless he was poor. And Granddad wasn't poor. It being a Saturday morning, there were already several men waiting while the man in the barber chair was tilted back for a shave with a steaming towel resting on his face. Everybody knew Granddad and he knew them. Granddad had been a rural mailman, delivering mail over the country roads, so he knew most everybody in town and out in the country, too. So everybody says, "Good Morning Steve, and how're ya doing?"

Granddad answers back, "Oh, I can't complain."

Dick Edding begins stropping his razor, slap, slap, slap, slap, as Granddad sits down on the long bench and I sit next to him, my feet dangling in the air.

"That Edward's boy you got there, Steve?"

"Yep. He's doing chores with me today."

"Well, that ought to keep him out of trouble. You know what they say, one boy can do a man's work, two boys are half a man, and three boys won't do any work at all."

"For certain that's true," says Bill Stout.

"How's the corn looking out your way?"

"If it rains in the next week, we'll have a decent crop."

Dick Edding lifts the towel from the man in the chair and lathers his face. I watch as the blade moves in swift short strokes under the chin and up the cheek. After each stroke the blade is wiped on a towel draped over the barber's left arm. Dick Edding holds the customer's nose between finger and thumb, little finger delicately raised, as he sweeps off the whiskers above the upper lip. When the shave is done, he shakes a squirt of sweet-smelling lotion onto the palm of a hand, puts the bottle back on the shelf, rubs his palms together, and applies aftershave to the customer's face in a few quick, noisy pats. Then takes a scissor and trims the customer's nose hairs.

"Next," Dick says as the customer gets up from his chair and takes a dollar from his wallet. It's 1944: the haircut is sixty cents; the shave is a quarter.

When I was in the fourth grade, I had a friend named Dick Nolan. Dick was a year or two older and, like me, had a younger brother. Dick was a head taller than me. With his blond hair combed back in a curl, I thought of him as handsome. Dick and his brother lived with their mother in the basement apartment of Dick Eddings's house on Main Street. The house was on two levels. The front door opened at the street level. The yard sloped sharply downward so that the door of the Nolans' apartment opened at the level of the grassy backyard. Mrs. Nolan did women's hair in the apartment. Her customers came around the house to that rear door to see her.

Jim and I visited the Nolan boys one afternoon to play in the backyard among the big shade trees. We were playing tag, running in all directions as fast as we could, when I ran headfirst into one of the steel clothesline posts. I bounced from it and fell flat onto my back. I was conscious, with stupefying pain in my head, and I couldn't breathe in or out. The Nolan boys and my brother Jim stood there look- ing at me as I lay, eyes open, not making a sound. Nobody knew that I couldn't breathe. It felt like minutes before my breath came back, although it might have only been a few seconds. I thought for sure I would die.

The reason I thought of Dick as a friend was that he told me things about his life and about other kids he had known before he moved to New London. Dick didn't say where it was, but he knew a boy who was a crack shot with a pellet gun. He said the more you pump it up, the more power the gun has. His friend could hit anything with a pellet gun, even at a distance. The boy with the pellet gun had a great dislike for a boy who had buckteeth. The boy with buckteeth had brown hair and always wore a blue shirt. He carried his lunch to school in a black box with a baling wire handle. And he always had a runny nose, spring, summer, fall, or winter. All the kids called him Bucky even though that wasn't his real name. No one had ever seen Bucky smile.

As Dick told me this, I realized that Bucky sounded like a kid in my class. Ronnie Powell's nose was always running. He never seemed to have a hankie, and he never seemed to smile or be happy. Always kind of whiney.

Dick said his friend had a bicycle and a paper route. Delivered the newspaper every morning before going to school. Made good money. That's how he'd bought the pellet gun. And he practiced shooting every day after school. He would try to get other boys to bet him that he couldn't hit something.

"Bet you a dime I can kill that pigeon," he would say.

"Bet you can't," someone would say. Then someone else would say, "A nickel says you can't." And then he'd kill the pigeon. It would flop to the ground right at his. feet. He'd pick it up by a wing and say, "You owe me a nickel." Pretty soon nobody would bet with him because he never missed. If you bet he'd miss, you'd lose your money.

"I was with him one day," Dick said. "We were looking up into the trees for something to shoot and stuff, and we saw Bucky sitting on a box in back of his uncle's hardware

store. 'Hey, Dick, bet you fifty cents I can shoot out
Bucky's front teeth.' 'That's impossible,' I told him. 'And
besides, who's got fifty cents?' 'You can owe me,' he said.

"And he pumped up the pellet rifle. Took a bead on
Bucky, just sitting there on that box. And took out one of
Bucky's front teeth. Bucky just sat there, couldn't understand what had happened. A couple of quick pumps, the rifle
was ready, and with a squeeze of the trigger, the other front
tooth was gone. Where Bucky'd had those big buck teeth
there was a gaping hole. People were mad as heck. Everybody knew there was only one person who could shoot like
that. So he had to pay for a set of false front teeth for Bucky.
Took all of his paper route money for a full year."

That was the story Dick told me. It seemed a little
unlikely. But I took Dick at his word because I had been
taught that you never, ever tell a lie.

It was a summer afternoon when Dick came out to the
farm. Boys don't have a plan when they are together. So
we didn't have anything in mind when we went into the
red barn in back of our house. The horse barn where Albert
Boss's sorrel draft mares were standing in the stalls. Dick
looked at the two horses.

"These are beauties," he said. "Let's take a ride."

"Well, we don't ride Albert's horses," I said.

Dick took a bridle down from the wall. "I ride all the
time on my dad's farm. He raises horses in Kentucky. It's
a big farm with hundreds of horses, big barns, and stables.
Huge pastures as far as you can see. There's a river running
through the farm. We ford it on horseback. There aren't any
farms like that around here."

64

I could just see that land and the herd of horses fording
the river, like in a Technicolor movie. I was filled with awe.
Dick slipped the bridle onto the head of a mare, placing the
bit in the horse's mouth. There was a saddle hanging on
the wall. I wasn't big enough to take it down. Dick lifted
it like nothing at all and swung it onto the horse's back,
cinched up the strap. As Dick led the mare into the barn lot,
I walked alongside. It didn't feel right that we were doing
this. I had never seen Albert ride his horses. But Dick was
so confident and sure of himself. He put his foot into the
stirrup and swung himself up into the saddle.

"What did I tell you,'" he said. "I've done this a thousand
times." And with that, Dick dug his heels into the mare's
side, and with a snap of the reins, said, "Giddy-up." The
horse rose up on its hind legs, like Trigger and Roy Rogers.

"Hoo baby," Dick said. "This is a spirited animal. I think
maybe this is enough for today." He swung his leg back
over the saddle and dropped to the ground. We walked
quietly back to the barn and put Albert's mare into the stall,
took off the saddle and bridle. Put everything back exactly
where it had been.

"Me and Dad go on long rides," Dick finally said. "But
there are times when you don't ride. Especially if the horse
doesn't feel like it."

Later I told Albert that we had saddled up his horse and
that it had reared up on its hind legs. Albert was angry.

"Who told you it was OK to put a saddle on my horse?
Those are draft horses, not riding horses. One of you might
have gotten hurt." Albert was a mild person. I had never
seen him mad before. Even so, he didn't cuss.

I told Dad that we had saddled Albert's horse. That Dick grew up riding horses and that his dad owned a big horse farm in Kentucky.

"Dick's dad is a welder. He lives over in Quincy. He's a drunk and doesn't have a pot to piss in." That was all Dad had to say about the matter. Dad didn't say Dick was a liar, but that was what he meant. I never said anything about it to Dick.

In the fall, during one afternoon's recess, I scrambled to the corner of the classroom and grabbed the ball and bat. Whoever had possession of these items could usually choose a team for a ballgame. But there were no takers, and I just stood there in the schoolyard leaning on the bat, ball in hand. Dick came up to me and said, "Baylis, give 'em to me." I handed him the bat and ball.

To my surprise, he tossed the ball into the air and swung the bat, sending the ball far out across the school ground, where it bounced and rolled into the yard across the street. I felt a sense of betrayal as I ran after the ball. What was going on? I picked up the ball. I had taken it out of the classroom, so it was my responsibility to bring it back. When I returned, Dick extended his hand as though expecting the ball, and I gave it to him. Then I stood in disbelief as he again casually tossed the ball and knocked it across the street.

I had been had. I felt like a dog chasing down the ball. I seethed with anger as I walked back with it. But when Dick asked for the ball a third time, I didn't seem to know how to refuse. I looked on in astonishment and confusion as he

again hit the ball across the street. Rage boiled up inside me.
This time he handed me the bat and turned to watch the ball
as it bounced in the street. I had been treated like a fool by
someone I had thought was my friend. I felt ashamed for
being so dumb, betrayed. My anger was such that I could
barely see.

I held the bat thinking, no don't hit him in the head, it
might kill him. I was just rational enough to know that I
didn't want to kill him. But the Bible doesn't say anything
about hurting someone. I calculated that if I hit Dick with a
nice horizontal swing, I might feel better. So I swung with all
I had as Dick stood, hands on hips, smugly gazing far across
the street, unaware of my rage, my sense of humiliation. If
Dick had intended to humiliate me, he had succeeded. But
maybe he hadn't; boys don't really plan. They just have
impulses. Maybe he just wanted to hit the ball and didn't
mean anything by it. All I knew is that I wanted to hurt him
like he had hurt me, or maybe a little more.

Boy, was Dick surprised when the bat slammed into his
wrist. Really surprised. He turned toward me holding his
swelling wrist in disbelief. He couldn't seem to understand
what might have gotten into me. But I felt much better. His
shock and misery were a salve for my wounds.

I had to account for my behavior to Miss Fanny, Miss
Christine, and Mrs. Lange. Miss Christine had been my
first- and second-grade teacher. Miss Fanny had taught me
in third and fourth grades. Mrs. Lange was my fifth-grade
teacher. She also taught sixth grade, Dick's class. The three
teachers sat in judgment as I explained what had happened.
Dick sat there as well, a wet towel wrapped around his

wrist. He seemed to have nothing to say. I felt almost self-righteous, slightly triumphant. I felt that my action had been justified. But I wasn't smiling.

Miss Fanny could deliver a nasty whack with the two-inch-wide hickory paddle she kept on her desk. I had seen her punishing Merle White for putting Johnny Briscoe's lunch box in the toilet. Merle had been made to lie across Miss Fanny's piano bench and received eight popping swats.

After they heard the details of my experience, there was a long silence. But I must have been understood. There was to be no paddling, just a week without recess. That was a punishment I could tolerate.

After that, I didn't speak to Dick anymore. He moved away a few months later, and I never saw him again.

Going to St. Louis

St. Louis was about a hundred miles away, and we would go there once in a while so Mom could shop. Dad went more often because he was on the board of the Sanitary Milk Producers Association. He would go to a board meeting every other month or so. It was about a two-hour drive. One time, Granddad went with us, and in the afternoon, I went with him to a movie. It was a black-and-white movie, and I couldn't make heads or tails of the story and really only liked color movies anyhow.

On another trip, Uncle Rec went with us. We drove past a farm with newly painted red barns and white-painted wooden fences.

"That man don't make his money farming. He ain't no farmer, because a farmer don't have time or money to paint a fence. Not even a gate." That sounded true to me. Uncle Rec didn't even have latches on his gates; all were held closed with a twist of baling wire.

One cold fall morning when we got to St. Louis, we went first to the Rexall Drugstore for the one-cent sale. Mom had the full-page ad from the Sunday *Post-Dispatch*. We went down the aisles looking for bargains as Mom looked up and down the page and scanned the coupons. I got one pack of Wrigley's spearmint gum for five cents and a second pack for one penny. The real problem with the sale was that after I bought the gum, I didn't have any money. I mostly never had money in my pocket anyway. If I wanted something, Mom might buy it. If I wanted a toy in the dime store, I would point it out to Mom, and if it wasn't more than a dime or fifteen cents, she might buy it. But if I got something, Jim would have to get something, too.

The most exciting place in St. Louis was Stix, Baer and Fuller, a huge department store with escalators. Jim and I would go to the sixth floor, where there was a whole department for official Boy Scout things: uniforms, camping equipment of all kinds. Just like in the army. It all looked so real and useful. Pocketknives, canteens, compasses. Each item clean and beautiful, all in glass display cases, carefully out of reach. We never got any of those things. All too expensive.

If we were in St. Louis in good weather, we might go to the zoo and see the elephant and snakes. There was a glass display case in the elephant house with the skull of the elephant that had gone mad and stomped on a six-year-old girl. The zoo had been giving children rides on the elephant. The little girl was next in line to ride and was mashed dead. I imagined her as a blonde with wiener curls, like Jolene Mitchell. Mom bought a book with pictures of the animals. The elephant skull was pictured in the book, but it didn't have a story about stomping the little girl or shooting the elephant.

One time when Mom and Dad went to St. Louis without us, they came back with gifts, two wind-up tanks with rubber treads and camouflage paint. Jim and I had been waiting up and began to test them right out of the box. They shot sparks from the gun turret as the tanks advanced across the floor. We put pillows on the floor for them to climb. That was right after the war.

Most always we went to the St. Moritz Grill in the late afternoon to meet up with Dad. Like all bars, the St. Moritz smelled of smoke and booze. I never liked the smell of either.

The family took a short trip to the Ozarks in 1950. We stopped at a restaurant and bar for supper late one afternoon. It was located near a stream flowing from an underground source, a lot of water flowing fast. Dad talked with the bartender about the water. Fifty-six thousand gallons a minute, the man behind the bar said. The place had a coin-operated game with a mechanical bear that traveled around a tree inside a little forest scene. The metal bear was painted brown and had a little glass window on each side of its belly. There was a rifle that shot a beam of light at the bear. If you aimed exactly right and hit the bear, it would roar fiercely, stand on its hind legs, and turn to run in the opposite direction. I only hit it once. But Dad could hit it again and again, making the bear turn back and forth, back and forth. The place smelled like a bar, and it was kind of dark. We had hamburgers. Dad had been drinking. That made Mom unhappy. It was not a happy day.

Whenever we returned home at night from a trip to St. Louis or even a PTA meeting, it would be dark. When we pulled into the driveway, we would see rabbits in the garden and the yard. That was a small treat. We didn't see them near the house during the day.

The Hole

It was back in the winter of 1953. I was in the sixth grade, and it was a Saturday morning when an event took place out in the back of that farm you could say was out of this world. Which was something Mom actually liked to say. It was about 10:00, and I was spreading manure on the corn field just east of the dairy barn. The sky was overcast to the north, and we were expecting rain. I was rushing the horses to get the work done when suddenly a gigantic explosion shook the ground, and the team pulling the spreader took off like two bats out of hell. The cow poop was a'flyin', and I had to hang on for dear life. When I got the horses stopped and under control and got myself calmed down, I noticed right away that there was a smell other than the cow manure in the air. Like burning steel. You could hear the putt-putt-putting of Dad's John Deere as it made its way across the field in back of the Old Perkins place.

Apart from the sound of the distant tractor, the air was strangely quiet. The horses twitched nervously, making their harness creak and tinkle. Then I heard the John Deere slow down and stop. Something had happened.

I tied the horses up at the fence and set out on foot for the back of the farm. That welded metal smell was every-where and it was starting to rain. As I stepped out of the woods that lined the old railroad track, I could see a small column of mist rising at the lower end of the large pasture, and Dad was climbing the fence near it.

What we found was the damnedest hole dug across the end of the north pasture right at the bottom of a slope. In the center of the hole was this hot rock about the size of an outhouse. The hole was dug at an angle and was about fifty feet long and thirty-some feet wide. And it was about fifteen feet deep right in the center where the big rock was. The grass around the edge was singed, and it was a good thing the rain had started falling or the heat from this thing would have set the field on fire.

Dad said he had sure never seen anything like this, and I said I hadn't either. Dad said he didn't know who threw this thing, and for sure he didn't want to meet up with the son of a bitch. He was just sure glad it had missed the barn. Dad had a sense of humor like that. He could find something funny in almost everything. Even the bad things. His brother, my Uncle Estes, had been helping to put up rafters on the new barn the summer before and had fallen right off the barn. Dad started laughing and just couldn't stop. Uncle Estes was mad as hell about being laughed at for falling off the barn, and he got in his Model T and plain left. Dad was still laughing and said he'd have laughed if the son of a bitch had killed himself. Dad laughed for about a full hour. I felt sorry for Uncle Estes and thought Dad should have made some kind of apology, and I guess he must have, seeing as how he and Uncle Estes got back to speaking and helping each other out again.

Dad walked around the rock, stepping on the ridge of the dirt mounded up around it. You couldn't get very close. It was red hot. And, of course, the cows started to come around after a bit and look at it, too. So there was the north pasture with me and Dad and about forty Jersey cows all standing around looking at a hot rock. Dad thought it was just damned funny.

I told Dad that I had read about this kind of thing in a science book at school and that they called this thing a meteorite. Which is a meteor that has landed. I began to make a whole explanation about it and said that people over at the university would be real interested in it and that our farm would be famous for being the place where this thing had come down. I was pretty excited by this prospect and was thinking about how Merle Johnson didn't have anything half as important or interesting on his dad's farm, which was twice as big as my dad's. And they had two covered silos!

Dad said that I wasn't to tell anybody about this rock and our hole. He didn't want them university fellows tramping around over the farm. It was bad enough in the fall when hunters—city fellas—came through the place. They didn't know how to climb a fence without damaging it.

"You got to climb with your feet right next to the post. If you try to climb in the middle, midway between the posts, you scrunch it down, and next thing you know, a cow is over the fence and your neighbor is pissed." Dad said the hole would make a fairly decent pond, and he'd actually been thinking of digging one right there anyhow.

As time passed, it turned out to be a first-rate pond. I swam in it after it filled up in the summer of '54. And for some reason, eight of our cows had twins the next spring. And the milk production was up about twenty percent that year. And although I didn't have any twins, my offspring have been unusual and pretty special. Certainly not average.

Mrs. Brown and the Walk Uptown

Mrs. Brown was my seventh-grade teacher, a single mother
of two who dressed in the straight skirts of the day with
matching jackets. It was 1953. She occasionally spoke
of her late husband. He had died unexpectedly of a heart
attack. She drove a '49 Ford, lived in Hannibal, and drove
the ten miles to New London and back each day, bringing
the two children with her.

While having little occasion to discuss politics in the
classroom, she did make known, more than once during
the year, her profound dislike of Harry S. Truman for
having fired General MacArthur, whom she regarded
as a true American hero and patriot. I had no opinion
about MacArthur, but my father, having taken the train to
Washington, D.C., for Truman's inauguration, and having
sat within about seventy-five feet of the ceremony—quite a
bit closer than county assessor Jack Briscoe, who perceived
himself to be well connected in Democratic political
circles—made Dad speak of Truman with great respect.
Also, Truman, like George Washington, was a Mason. Dad
was a thirty-second-degree Mason and Grand Master of
the local Masonic lodge. So I did have a generally positive
feeling about the thirty-third president, but I never made a
point of making my preferences in the matter known.

These were the years in which the new grade school was
being built at the edge of town next to the Cerf Bros. Bag
Company factory and the water tower. The new gymnasium, having been completed before the classrooms, housed

the physical ed classes, so students were being shuttled from the old school to the new gym by bus, usually operated by Merle Winnaker, the vocational Ag teacher. This is not a matter of great importance, except to say that things were in flux.

The new building would be an exciting place. Opulent by comparison with the old red brick thing right across the street from a blacksmith, whose trip-hammer we could hear from time to time as he shaped a piece of red-hot iron. The old building, containing all eight grades and high school, was only one long block from the Ralls County Courthouse and two blocks from Highway 19, which bisected New London.

For some reason Mrs. Brown decided that the seventh grade would make a brief walking tour of the business district, to gain, perhaps, an insight into the workings of the community. It was only a short walk, and honestly, we already knew where things were because we lived there, but she was from out of town. For me the only really new experience was seeing the linotype machine with which John Porter Fisher, Sr., set type for each weekly issue of the *Ralls County Record*, for which he was editor, publisher, manager, and salesclerk. This is important because my first published work appeared in the December 1946 "Letters to Santa" column.

We did stop in at the Co-Op, where you could get all kinds of feed, seed, fuel, and farm supplies. You could bring in a load of grain and have it milled and mixed with supplements. There were assorted agricultural chemicals like DDT, H2-4-d, and d-Con to kill rats. Stuff like that. Cousin Roberta was the bookkeeper. It turned out that an outside audit revealed that she had embezzled slightly over $4,000, quite a sum of money. To save our family name, Uncle Rec was called upon to reimburse the Co-Op, so no charges were filed. In a small town, things get worked out. Uncle Rec was a bachelor, still had every dollar he had ever earned. I always wondered why he only gave me a quarter for Christmas; I thought it should have been a dollar.

We walked past the movie theater. I had gone there one recent afternoon with my brother Stevie and Bob German, the projectionist. We went upstairs to the projection booth. I had never been to the balcony before. I was shocked to discover that the balcony where Black people sat had wooden benches instead of individual theater seats. I commented that they must have had to sit separately. He looked away and said nothing.

We visited the post office, old hat for me, Dad being the postmaster. I often went there after school if Mom was in town to do some shopping. A few months previously, as I sat in back where mail was sorted reading *Popular Science* magazine, of which there always seemed to be several recent copies, I observed my younger brother John, a second grader, to be very focused and busy writing on a sheet of paper, then folding it, followed by a flurry of stapling. I watched as he placed the completed document where it would be noticed. Drawn to it by the sheer energy of its creation, I read the cover: "Top Secret—Do Not Open," which was stapled on all edges. I dutifully tore it open as he watched with a sly smile on his face. The message read: "Fuck Shit Damn Hell." All the bad words he knew how to spell. I was impressed by his audacity and imagination.

Next door to the post office was the Made-Rite Potato Chip factory, run by Slim Williams, whose jaw had been broken three years earlier by Arlen German, proprietor of the dry cleaners, for taking in clothes for a competing dry cleaner from Hannibal, but that's another story. Slim went from one of his several skills to another. He had built the room that became my bedroom onto the west side of our house in 1947, laid new oak flooring, and installed our life-changing, first-ever indoor toilet with bathtub and shower. Slim's wife was our route's school bus driver. She had slapped the twelve-year-old son of Uncle Rec's hired hand for uttering words of disrespect in response to a perceived insult. The next morning the hired hand was waiting for the bus holding a shotgun. He told her to keep her God-damned hand off his kids. Of course, the sheriff had to drop by and have a chat with the hired hand. That was the end of it. The potato chip factory was astonishingly small, twelve by thirty feet. Two people worked scooping chips into small Made-Rite labeled bags and stapling them closed. No mystery there. We were in and out in five minutes. No samples were given; business wasn't all that good.

Next door was Doreman's Harness Shop, closed on account of Mr. Doreman having been knocked down by an intoxicated dolt across the street in front of Pinefetty's Bar on a Sunday afternoon the year before. Mr. Doreman fell backward into the street. Died of a concussion on the spot. There was a coroner's inquest but no charges filed. I should have seen the whole thing—it happened right in front of where I was sitting in our Hudson—but I was unaware, listening to the Sunday New York Philharmonic broadcast on the radio. Mr. Doreman had made a full set of harnesses for Dad's team of dapple-gray mares about the time I was in the first grade. One of the tugs broke during the horse-pulling contest at Center, Missouri, and Nelly, Dad's favorite fell to her knees. Dad was terribly upset; his team looked like it would have taken first place. Mr. Dorman was also terribly upset about it, remade the tugs at no cost. But the horse-pulling contest was over.

Farther down the street was the Kroger store, but everybody already knew about that, too. The coffee grinder was near the front of the store, so the place was often permeated with the agreeable smell of freshly ground coffee. And there was Naylor's Fountain and Drugstore, where Dad had coffee and toast every morning after getting the mail out. Then there was Thomas's Hardware, where they sold plumbing supplies and tools, Youngstown-brand steel kitchen cabinets, toilets and sinks, copper pipe, various kinds of cable, wire, rope, all manner of electrical fuse boxes, circuit breakers and such, and shovels, picks, axes, corn knives, assorted pocketknives, many types of woodworking tools and sharpening stones, and bolts and screws.

A couple of years later I would work the entire summer at Thomas's Hardware as Bud Stroud's helper. Bud was a plumber, electrician, and what have you. He could do most anything. I enjoyed working with him. He had a few interesting things to tell me about his time in the U.S. Navy during World War II. He worked in the confined space of the torpedo room of a submarine. It made me think I would have suffered from claustrophobia, but he handled it just fine. He told me that the torpedo fuel was one hundred percent pure grain alcohol. He and his mates would cut the stuff with water and get loaded from time to time. Bud was a pretty straightforward guy. Honest, hardworking family man. We installed a toilet, Youngstown enameled steel kitchen cabinets, and new sink at a home in Center; installed an indoor bathroom out southwest of town for a World War I vet who seemed to live on tobacco juice. Spat into a can all the time. The old guy seemed pretty spent to me but kind of lively at the same time. Given his condition, a real talker.

We also delivered bottles of propane gas to customers, removing the empty tank and attaching a full one. We delivered gas south of town one afternoon to a place where the kitchen was a lean-to at the back of the house. These were poor people, poor like I didn't know existed in Ralls County. I couldn't quite believe it. We didn't go inside the house; Bud said there was an inch of dirt on top of the wood floors, that's how ignorant these folks were.

Thomas's Hardware had been operated by Mr. Thomas and his wife, Idella. I had only one occasion to meet Mr. Thomas. He had been asked to coach a local Little League team on the grounds behind the new school. I showed up, same as a dozen and a half others roughly my age. While pitching part of an inning, I was hit in the chest by a line drive, a painful, disorienting, and humiliating experience. Mr. Thomas then assigned me to play first base. The very next play was ordinary enough: a bouncing ball inside the third base line, caught by the third baseman, thrown to me at first. I missed the throw, it hit me in the mouth. I was a mess. Mr. Thomas drove me home, bleeding, bruised, dazed, and twice humiliated as I was, just those two miles west of town on Highway 19. He pulled into the driveway and stopped. As I got out he told me to take it easy and rest for a while. That was the end of my baseball career. My life options were being whittled down right before my eyes.

Mr. Thomas had a heart attack and died a few months later. So it was Idella Thomas for whom I was working, a hardnosed store manager who promptly rejected my request for a raise midway through the summer of my apprenticeship.

"You're not learning fast enough where things are," she said. "People come in and you can't tell them where fuses are. You have a ways to go." She was paying me sixty-five cents an hour, and I was trying to put together enough money to buy a Bozak speaker for the hi-fi I was building.

A manufacturer's rep for plumbing supplies came through every few weeks. Bud Stroud said the man slept over in Idella's apartment upstairs above the store. I asked how he knew. He said when it snowed overnight, there wouldn't be any snow under the Cadillac parked in front of the store.

Farther down the street was Lonnie Nichols's liquor store, where Dad bought his whiskey, mostly Old Crow. He kept a bottle in the post office bathroom medicine cabinet, one under the kitchen sink at home, one in the smokehouse, and one on the back porch. Probably kept Lonnie in business. We didn't go in there.

We did stop in at the Ralls County State Bank. Aunt Sue, Mom's sister, was the head cashier, pretty much managed

the bank except for making loans. She ran a tight ship with
never a slip-up. Dad had introduced her to the banker right
after she finished high school in 1945. Dad was, after all,
on the bank's board of directors and had been one of the
dozen initial investors, which is not to suggest that there
was any favoritism involved or that we were rich. Aunt
Sue had a bit of luck, but so did the bank. She stayed there
her whole working life; never had a single other job. Many
years later, long after I had fled for other places and Aunt
Sue had retired, her daughter came to work for the bank
as a teller. She began secretly making weekend loans to
herself from the cash drawer for her vocation as a riverboat gambler. That worked for her until her winning streak
ended and she couldn't replenish the borrowed cash before
business opened on Monday morning. It turns out that I
come from a family of embezzlers.

We didn't visit Hunter Hulse's feed store opposite the
courthouse front either. There wasn't much to Hunter's
place: the south wall was lined with stacks of various kinds
of ground feed and feed supplements. Hunter's was sort of
an unofficial Democratic headquarters, an institution where
matters large and small were endlessly discussed. There
was an American flag and the flag for the state of Missouri
and pictures on the wall of assorted Democratic senators,
congressmen, and governors and, of course, Franklin
Delano Roosevelt and Harry S. Truman. All signed, some
with personal best wishes to Hunter. In the back of the
store were several old round oak dining tables, the kind
with claw feet around a center column. Old men came there
every day to play pinochle or cribbage. My grandfather had

played here. Dad would stop in to say hello. There were always six or eight old-timers. They swapped stories and commented on the world passing by, enjoying one another's company. Once in a while somebody would come in and buy some feed.

At the end of the block, also facing the courthouse, was Bob Bonnell's garage and Ford dealership, with its inventory of three new cars. Several of the employees were Black men. I was with Dad one evening near Christmas time. The garage was closed, and the men were shooting craps. Dad had been drinking that evening and had a half pint of Old Crow in his pocket. He took out his bottle and passed it around. Dad was a man ahead of his time in certain ways. The class didn't visit Bonnell's either. Everybody knew what a garage was about.

We went through the courthouse. Looked into the assessor's office and the county registrar's office, where we said hello to Virgil McGowan. Mom said it was Virgil who was in bed with Dad's first wife when Dad unexpectedly returned home one afternoon. Of course, I didn't learn about that until fifty years later. Upstairs we stepped into the grand courtroom, which looked pretty much as it must have the first time a gavel called a court into session almost a century before. It was rather stately in a modest way, with the white walls, the American flag, and the Missouri state flag at either side of the bench. A large bookcase full of ancient law books stood against the south wall. I wondered if anyone ever consulted them.

Down the hall, directly in back of the courtroom, was the Selective Service office, run by Mrs. Hoffmeyer, Becky

Shelburn's grandmother. For some reason never known to me, Becky, who was in my class, had always lived with her grandmother. There must have been some brief moment in the second or third grade when I had a crush on Becky. I did ask her out on a date when I was in high school. It was a triple date, with brother Jim and Sandra Sue Lemon, odd and strange. We stopped off at the Lemon residence on the way home from the movie. Their home was at the end of a long driveway, and the car mysteriously ran out of gas halfway there. I was unaccustomed to such ruses, and it took a while for me to pick up on the theme. It didn't matter. As unaggressive as I was, my cordiality was sternly rejected. Soon enough, the car miraculously started, and we all had apple pie in the Lemons' kitchen.

We exited the courthouse through the back door and walked as a group to the sheriff's office across the street next to the Methodist Church. The sheriff greeted us warmly, spoke to us for a couple of minutes, then showed us through a steel door into the jail, one medium-sized room with two cells to the left side. I was the last one to the door, and for some reason, utterly without forethought or malice, as a joke, I stepped back and closed the door. It was a solid steel door with a small window. The door clicked when it closed, and I ran out the front door, thinking it was a funny thing to have done. But the door was locked and the sheriff was inside with the entire seventh-grade class and Mrs. Brown. And although the sheriff had a key, he could not reach the latch. I had stepped outside into the lawn to bask in the sunlight of my cleverness. Pretty soon there was yelling for me to come back and set everyone free. The sheriff was pretty embarrassed. Since nobody was injured or anything, I thought it was kind of a cool thing to have done. But Mrs. Brown was really pissed off. The walk back to the schoolhouse was very quiet, and the incident was never spoken of again.

Joyce

She was a redhead and probably possessed all the traits attendant thereto. A rebel. A fireball. To sum it up, she was already a woman not to be trifled with. Her name was Joyce. When she was thirteen years old and I was twelve, we had a remarkable encounter in which her impulsiveness and creativity were revealed.

The event was small on the scale of human events, and there is no record of it written anywhere, except here. It was really quite innocent, but at the time it seemed deviant and terrible, and somehow just a bit wonderful, too: a partial lifting of the veil of innocence—with no apparent ill effects.

It was an ordinary day pretty much like the others that preceded it and the ones that would follow. This was small-town America in the mid-1950s. Communists and the evil of drink were just about the worst things to worry about at the time. And success in sports was the goal most visibly sought after. Sex existed, but it was a figment of my imagination. I didn't even know that masturbation was really possible. I had heard of it but never experienced it. Because sex was so far from my real experience, it simmered away in my brain waiting for biology to turn the fire up.

The red brick school was a two-story structure with a bell on top and a flagpole out front. The front lawn was grassy in the spring and muddy in winter. Through prodigious efforts by my parents and others, a bond issue had been passed, and a new grade school building, with a

wondrous gymnasium, had been erected out at the edge
of town, right next to the water tower and Cerf Bros. Bag
Company. The gym seemed almost too grand and gigantic
to be real. All students went to the new building for physical education. To travel the nine blocks, we boarded a
big yellow school bus to be driven to the gym by the phys
ed coach. I can't remember why both boys and girls were
going to the gym at the same hour, but on this particular
day it must have been co-ed.

After the event to be related, I was called to appear
before several of my teachers to give an account of what
had happened. All the teachers had known me since I was
in the first grade. I was generally considered to be a "good
boy" from a family established in the community for most
of a century. Whereas Joyce Griffith was an outsider. Child
of a broken family, she had come to live with an uncle. She
was a city girl. But she had not even a whiff of sophisti-
cation, a fact that seemed confirmed by the gaps between
her teeth. She was a tomboy, tough and outspoken, wore
jeans and played baseball, as did many of the girls. There
were no dress codes because most students had farm chores
when they got off the school bus.

The day in question was in early spring. Warm enough
that we were dressed in shirtsleeves. It was a cloudless
afternoon, and you could hear corn being milled at the
co-op feed store two blocks away. Across the street from
where the bus parked was my cousin Virge's house. She'd
lived there fifty-plus years. Once in a while before school,
I'd go chat with her. And across in front of the school was
a blacksmith's shop where I had watched the building of

a beautiful new wagon when I was in the second grade. Horse-drawn. Painted red and yellow. From the schoolroom window we had seen the smith pump the forge.

Coach Geiger, our bus driver for the day, had not yet come out of the school when I climbed aboard and took a seat near the middle of the bus. Several other students were already seated near the front. Suddenly there was a mad rush out the schoolhouse door—a bevy of kids led by Joyce. Stronger and faster than the others, she was on the bus in a flash. In a display of cunning and bravado, she grabbed the handle, slamming the door shut in the faces of the rest of the pack, locking them out. It was an innocent trick. They responded by banging on the door and yelling to be let in.

In those days I was a loudmouth and, in retrospect, a self-righteous butthole.

"C'mon, Joyce, open the door and let 'em in!" I yelled. She was playing a game, and I wanted to throw cold water on it. So she shouted back, as those outside kicked at the door, "KISS MY ASS!"

It was about as rude a thing as any of us said to anyone else. And in fact it was a shocking thing for a girl to say; it was more the kind of thing a guy would say to another guy. Nobody except Larry Michlan would even want to kiss another guy's ass, but Larry was what was called queer in those days, although I hadn't figured that out yet.

What struck me as especially glorious about this challenge from Joyce was that I knew the antidote for the poisonous phrase. The final come-back, for which there was no known countermeasure.

Standing in the aisle of the big yellow bus, I savored the incredible ultimate comeback on my tongue. I would spit it out like young wine. Life had heaped on me a multitude of humiliations, and I needed a triumph. That phrase, "kiss my ass." So crisp and to the point. But I knew that my reply would put her down.

"Kiss my ass, you say?" I didn't think up the reply, I had heard it. But I knew it was effective. So I loosed my bolt of lightning. "Make it bare!"

To my utter astonishment, and that of everyone else on the bus, Joyce turned to me and casually unzipped her jeans. They were boy's jeans with the zipper in front. Looking directly into my eyes, a faint smile on her lips, she slowly and confidently pushed the Levi's down. Down over her curvy hips, revealing green nylon panties with black and yellow stripes. Carefully, her thumbs stretched the panties and slid them down slowly as she looked me straight in the eyes, knowing that she had won.

My jaw dropped as I looked on in absolute awe. At last a tuft of curly red hair peeked over the panties at me. Time had ceased to exist. The noise of the protesting students fell away. I gasped in astonishment. I was twelve years old and I had never seen this particular view of a girl before. I wasn't even capable of fantasizing about a girl partially exposing herself, and I had done it with a phrase. But she had won the battle of wits. She had proven that she was smarter and certainly more courageous than I. I could never have exposed myself to a girl on a bus, in front of other people. I just couldn't have done it. But even in my defeat there was a victory for me. Joyce had shown me a tuft of red hair. In so doing she had both defeated and rewarded me. Triumph and defeat in the same moment delivered by this demon goddess.

I'm sure there were other, less cautious boys who would have lunged for Joyce's beautiful thirteen-year-old ass. Carl Stout would have done it. Once when he and several other of the older boys were holding a seminar on sex in the school library, Carl had posed the following hypothetical question:

"You know what I'd do if there was a naked woman lying right here on this table?" Well, I didn't know what he'd do, and for that matter I had no idea what I would do other than look at her. Nobody else seemed to know what to do either. "Well, I'd fuck her. Right here on the table." And I was sure he would have. I think we all made the assumption that a woman lying naked on a library table would, of course, want to fuck Carl Stout. (Carl was known to cut the bottoms out of his pockets so he could play with himself during school. What an imagination!) Carl had even taken his penis out once when the teacher was out of the room to display it for one of the girls. You wouldn't think of him as a sensitive and tasteful person. But you would say he had balls.

Joyce never had anything to do with Carl Stout. She finally married Floyd Leak. And they had a boy they named Cletus. Cletus Leak. The Leaks were a family of gigantic men: men of immense proportions and vision. Each had been put on a tractor to work the fields from the age of six. Together they farmed over two thousand acres, back when that was quite a bit of land. They were hard workers. And a bit rowdy. Floyd and Buddy got a little drunk in a bar over in Center and threw a patron through the front window, Western movie–style. So you can see Joyce had hitched up with a pretty tough hombre. Mom told me that Floyd and Joyce fought a lot. On one occasion Joyce threw a skillet of hot gravy at Floyd. It missed. Shortly after that Joyce left Floyd, taking with her Cletus and the color TV.

I wish her well and thank her for that wonderful view of things to come. I never made it with a redhead, but then I never had anyone throw a pan of hot gravy at me, either.

The Girl in the Sousaphone Box

It was the first year that our rural school district had a band.
The basketball coach had a brand new '54 Buick and I had
a new cornet. The inside of the cornet case was incredibly
plush and reeked with a pungent newness. The excitement
of possessing this splendid thing was almost as overwhelm-
ing as the disappointment at not being able to make a musical sound the first time I tried to play it.

The notion of having a school band was grand and heady.
It had always seemed that other schools had a band but not
us, and now we would have one. The Band Mothers was
formed to raise money for uniforms. They held bake sales
in the front window of Thomas's Hardware store. They held
a chili supper and asked for donations. And finally, after
great effort, they were able to buy some other school's cast-
off uniforms, which had the smell of aged wool and evap-
orated sweat. The buttonholes were frayed, and the little
hooks that held the coats closed at the collar needed repair.
But we forgave all imperfections. The uniforms seemed the
very essence of splendor and importance.

When the fall festival came, the band hadn't yet learned
to march, so we rode seated in folding chairs on a flatbed
truck, the cab decorated with crepe paper pom-poms and
streamers, the bed skirted with bunting. We played badly,
but everyone cheered. We were the new school band.

It was the same fall festival parade that I had been in
many times before, with my dog and decorated tricycle
when I was four. Later, dressed as Li'l Abner on a float with

my friend Zoe as Daisy Mae portraying a shotgun wedding. And once as Uncle Sam on the post office float.

When I was very young, I attended a community sing at the county courthouse. A whole bunch of people from town gathered there together singing. There was a centennial in 1958 to celebrate the building of the courthouse. It was a hot August night, and I wore my Uncle Rec's beige double-breasted wool suit to escort Zoe, who wore an elegant lacy dress with a bustle. We marched across the courthouse lawn and up the sandstone steps of the Greek temple courthouse.

There was something about those community events that reverberated in my mind. We were acting out rituals that had ceased to be completely viable, the final gasps of a dying era. I had seen images of Main Street from earlier years when there were more people. There had been a Kroger store, a five-and-ten-cent store, a dry goods store. These were gone. The year 1956 saw the last fall festival with carnival rides and a livestock show. The movie theater had closed in the summer of 1955. Everybody was content to watch television.

All of this was the background for a time when I was an uncomfortable outsider, a pudgy and lonely adolescent trying to find meaning, companionship, and a place to be comfortable in the world. Sex was something that boys talked about with boys. They didn't discuss it with parents or anyone who knew. The mechanics of sex were manifest everywhere in rural life. Some animal or other was always in rut somewhere. Cows in the barn lot. Horses in the pasture. One afternoon two dogs were humping in the street outside the band room window, coupled but unable to disconnect.

Everything I knew about sex was anecdotal. It was condemned in church on the one hand and sanctified on the other. Sexiness was glorified in pin-up calendar photos on the walls of various garages. All in all, it added up to making sex very interesting. But I didn't understand why my friend Malcolm thought it was sexy to see some pictures of naked boys. He had some and wanted to show them to me. I failed to understand the point. Whatever it was that boys might be able to do with other boys in the sexual sense didn't seem interesting.

Someone brought an "eight-page bible" to school when I was in the second grade. It showed Olive Oyl coupled with Popeye and Wimpy and various other cartoon characters. It was dirty, terrible, exciting, forbidden, and really interesting. I had dreams in those times of a forest in the school-yard with all the teachers and all the girls tied to the trees. I could examine and probe the girls to see how they were made. This would take place in the afternoon on a warm, sunny day. No one would speak.

When I was six years old, I had dreams about being in a small, dark house with Jolene, who at the time seemed to me incredibly beautiful and unattainable. I kissed her on the cheek after she played a piano solo at church. At school, in an effort to get her attention, I had put a small and wonderful wind-up toy truck down the back of her dress. The spring mechanism had entwined itself in the gorgeous blond wiener curls that tumbled from her head and became firmly attached to the back of her neck. I used up an entire recess period trying to untangle it. In the dream about the small house, I was with Jolene and tried find out how she was made. Unlike me, she did not have one penis. She had two.

It was on the evening of the Band Mothers' chili supper that I made a sexual discovery that left a bitter taste. The school was small and located in two buildings. The lower contained the band rehearsal room and the agriculture shop room where the supper was being held. The older two-story brick building was open but empty. The band had performed for the chili supper, and kids were outside playing in the schoolyard. Parents were in groups talking. For some reason, I went to the small library room on the second floor of the old brick building. The room was about twelve by twelve feet and contained some books. But it was also being used as the storage room for the large band instruments that weren't taken home. The snare and base drums, the glockenspiel. And the sousaphone.

In the corner of the room was the box for the sousaphone, a shipping crate about the size of a small refrigerator resting on its side. Had I seen a girl and two of the boys go up there? I must have. As I entered the room, I heard a girl's voice whispering, protesting; held in, desperate. There was scuffling and movement in the box. The room was dark, and outside I could hear the sound of children at play. Inside the box, the pleading whisper and crying. The crying of stifled tears. I stood just inside the door listening, drawn by the mystery of the forbidden. And dark.

When the two boys emerged, they looked at me without speaking and left. Slowly, I walked around the box to see for myself some evidence of what might have taken place. Inside was a girl two years older than myself. I had known

her since the second grade. In a small town, you knew
everyone. She was kneeling huddled against the side of the
box and holding the back of her blouse which was unbut-
toned. And she looked at me with tears streaming down her
cheeks.

I said nothing and neither did she. What could I say?
I had been drawn to that room by the same curiosity and
urges as had her tormentors. I knew that she had been
violated. I sensed that she couldn't cry out. In small towns,
girls get blamed for what happens to them. Why else had
she gone up there? She had wanted to be with boys and had
sneaked up here with them. She had taken a risk, and her
trust had been violated. Always the outsider, I had experienced violated trust. The treachery of brutal boys. I had
played with boys, only to have them strike out and hurt me
on a whim I simply could not comprehend. They had the
compassion of reptiles. But I, too, lacked compassion.

I just looked at her, compelled by my sexual curiosity
to see what I could. I think I was stunned by her tears.
By the reality of the moment. She was a plump girl with
large breasts. She was lonely and alone. Isolated from her
younger brother. Her father had a vending machine business; jukeboxes, pinball machines. He was never around. I
never knew her mother. This may have been her first humiliation. But there came to be others. The sheriff would find
her in the company of a group of Black men and take her
home, saying that the father should look out for her.

In later years, I heard that she had married an older man,
that she had a couple of children. That she was happy. I
hope that is true. Because small towns can be cruel. Even

as a boy I knew that. I knew also that I had been an accomplice in the small-town darkness of that room, in that room with the books and musical instruments. In the proximity of all the symbols of art and culture that my hometown possessed, a child had suffered, and I had stood by with eyes to see but no voice to speak.

A Hundred Years of Dogs

My people are dog men. Granddad had dogs. Dad had dogs. And I had two. Granddad raised foxhounds all his life and this is what he told me.

"Me and Mr. Richard Fry and Mr. Ray Kahn, and the Strodes, and some others—we'd meet 'bout when it was a'gittin on to dark. Maybe out on the old Dougmore place. Maybe on the hill up back of the Wilson farm. We'd set up some camp chairs, a couple of lanterns. Sometimes we'd gather for a couple of days to run the dogs and talk. After dark we'd loose the dogs. The young fellas would follow the dogs and there'd be a bunch of the dogs, too, I tell you. Maybe fifteen, maybe twenty. Them dogs would just go.

"We'd sit around and listen to the dogs run. You know your own dog and you know your friends' dogs. They make some kind of racket. If you been running dogs for some part of your life, hearing 'em is just as good as seeing 'em. You can tell the minute they find a fox's trail because the dogs are talking to you. If you know how to listen you know which dog is out front and which one is close behind. And you know these farms like the back of your own hand. Mr. Fry might say, 'They're crossing the branch now.' We say things like that just to be saying it. We all know exactly where those dogs are. The dogs are telling us.

"Now my best dog was Rowdy. Most dogs couldn't lay a candle to him. And he sired some fine pups. There wasn't a better dog anywhere round these parts and he was a well-known dog. People knew about Rowdy in three states. Fact is somebody bothered to steal him once and I figured he was gone for good. I'd looked everywhere around this neck of the woods, so I knew he wasn't 'round here. Then I got a letter from a foxhunter down near Springfield. Now that's about five hundred miles from here. Said he'd seen my dog. Absolutely sure it was my Rowdy. Well I was sitting on the porch one hot Sunday afternoon and ol' Rowdy came limping right into the yard. He was thin as could be and hurting. The pads on his paws were practically worn out. He was a sight. He just lay down right there at my feet and panted. I was careful to put him back onto his feed slow. In a couple of months Rowdy was back to health and he lived to a ripe old age. He was a fine dog."

Often after a hunt a dog might be missing. You wouldn't think so, but they do get lost, or sometimes, caught in a fence. I was with Granddad one hot summer morning in 1946. We were walking up the gravel driveway to Clara Briscoe's house. Granddad pulled a white handkerchief from his hip pocket, removed his straw hat, and wiped the sweat from his forehead. Cicadas were sawing in the dry grasses.

"Somebody's got a dead cow," Granddad said as he pointed to a column of circling buzzards. When we got to Clare's back porch, she said she hadn't seen no dogs, but she'd let him know if any came by. She gave us each a cold Pepsi in the twelve-ounce bottle, and it was really good. It made Granddad give a loud belch, and I laughed.

After Granddad retired from farming, he moved to town. In back of his garage he had built a high-fenced pen for his dogs. All his life he'd kept hounds, bred them, and sold them. In town he had only seven. Rowdy was long gone. These had names like Buck and Ben, Nicked Ear, Tough Boy, Scrappy. In a shed next to the garage stood a fifty-gallon drum of deep-fried pork rinds called cracklings, a barrel of bran, and a barrel of rolled oats. Every morning Granddad would cook a huge pot of what he called mash. He had a coal oil stove in there, and you could smell that batch of dog food all around the neighborhood.

One of the things you have to know about farm dogs is they don't come into the house. Maybe the back porch when it rains or snows. Maybe the basement if a bitch is having pups and it's freezing in the barn. But never in the house. That would have been true for Old Jeff, Dad's favorite dog ever. Dad was never interested in hounds. But in his hunting years he always had some kind of bird dog. This is what Dad would say to anybody who'd listen.

"Jeff was a red Irish setter. Best hunting dog I ever had. I don't think anybody had ever owned a better hunting dog. If you went hunting with other dogs, Jeff honored their points. He'd stand on a point for ten minutes if need be, waiting for you to be ready. That dog was something else. If you shot a duck, he was right in the water after that duck. There just wasn't anything he couldn't do.

"We lived across the road in those days. The house was only sixty feet from the highway, and there wasn't any fence around the yard. If my two-year-old son started walking toward the road, the dog would go and lie right down in front of him. And if the boy went around Jeff, why he'd just get right up and put himself between the

boy and the road again. You never saw anything like it.
And if Sarah couldn't find the boy, she'd call Jeff and the
boy would come following the dog. It was just uncanny.
That Jeff was some dog, I tell you."

Bird dogs love to hunt. And they love to ride in a car,
even the trunk. Dad would open the trunk and the dogs
would jump right in. Dad and one or two of his favorite
hunting buddies would leave early in the morning so they'd
be in the field at sunrise. After they'd got the limit, they'd
come home for breakfast: eggs, bacon, coffee, and whiskey.
It broke Dad's heart when Jeff got run over on the highway.
Just broke his heart.

There was one exception to the no-dog-in-the-house
rule. Frisky was a small dog, not the sort you'd have on
a farm, and the only one we ever let in the house proper.
It was a small fox terrier that Cousin Nettie Weaver left
with us when she moved to Florida. Sometime in the night
you would hear Frisky's toes click-click-click across the
living room floor, then he'd jump up on the rocking chair.
It would squeak and rock for a moment. Then, except
for Dad's snoring, the house would be silent again. In
the fall festival parade, Mom dressed my brother and me
as clowns. Frisky wore a ruffled collar and a cute little
pointy hat. His look was one of forbearance. Frisky got
run over on the road, too. That broke my heart. I was four
at the time.

The truth is Mom never really liked dogs. And she
especially didn't like the black lab mix Dad got when I was
six. The fact is I didn't like the dog either. Mom said he

was the kind of dog that would suck eggs and run rabbits; she would say that about someone who was dishonest, too, because that's what dogs do.

When Dad was away on a trip for a few days having a good time somewhere and Mom was left home with us boys, she used the dog to send Dad a message. All us boys with Mom walked across the pasture to the abandoned railroad track. I led the dog with a rope around its neck. My older half-brother carried the 12-gauge. No one was saying anything. Except for the sound of a distant tractor, meadow birds, and the movement of our clothes, it was quiet and eerie but exciting, too, in a really sickening way.

I now know that Mom was really pissed at Dad. She managed her household with more constraint than necessary. But every year, Dad spent money to travel to the National Postmasters' Convention. He always drank a lot while there, and probably did some things he shouldn't have. Mom tied the dog to a tree, where he was summarily executed. We boys went by the place every few weeks over that summer to watch the dog turn into leather and gradually melt into the soil. It was a long time before anything grew on that spot. Many years later, Mom and I collected an armload of morel mushrooms there. She said it was a fairy circle.

Fifty years later my own family acquired a dog named Molly, the gift of a friend who found her cowering under a bush while walking her two dogs. My wife, Kathy, had an image of the dog even before it was described to her. Kathy was kind of mystical about certain things. When we went to the friend's house to meet Molly, the beast immediately put her chin on my daughter's knee. I didn't want a dog; they're expensive to keep, you have to make arrangements if you go away, and they have to be walked four times a day even if it's raining cats and dogs and water is ass-deep in the streets. So I said no. But I am merely the agent of other people's intentions in my household, so the dog came home with us.

Molly's spirit had been broken. She walked with her tail down, ears limp, a down-dog look about her. And she was skinny to boot. The second day, she dug a hole under the fence and ran away. Kathy went into freak-out mode. I said there was nothing to be done, that the dog would probably come back. Where else would she get fed? Molly returned in a couple of hours having checked out the local geography.

Ours was not an easy relationship. After a few weeks of taking her for walks, I decided I could let her off the leash, thinking that she would walk alongside. I was wrong. She took off like a bat out of hell, running into yards through the bushes around the edges of the houses, and it took some doing to get her back on the leash. It took me a while to understand that she was part border collie: she was looking for sheep.

Gradually Molly began to be part of the family and walked with her fringed ears perked up, her tail waging in the breeze. As time passed she became essential to the conduct of our domestic affairs.

Caring for Molly became my daughter, Sarah's, responsibility. Sarah has Down syndrome; she is developmentally handicapped. She walked Molly around the neighborhood mornings and evenings, picking up the dog's droppings in a plastic bag and giving the household a detailed scat report. When the ground was wet with dew or rain, Sarah washed Molly's paws on returning. She would say "towel" and Molly would assume a sitting posture in the middle of a towel spread on the floor. Molly tolerated having her feet dunked one by one into a bucket of water and wiped dry, all the while with an attitude of "well, if you must." Sarah spoke of Molly as having "dog emotions," referred to her as a "dog person," and would sometimes quote Molly as having expressed a particular thought.

At that time our household included my mother-in-law, who came to live with us after having had a significant stroke. Some months later she had another of her TIAs, tiny strokes that progressively led to senile dementia. That morning we arose to find Mom lying on the floor next to her bed, the sheets pulled down from the bed onto her. As we helped Mom back into bed, Molly jumped onto the bed, lay down beside the woman and for several hours refused to leave her side, as if bound to her in some highly obligatory way. My wife took this kind of thing for granted. I was astonished and had to completely reconsider what the dog was about.

As I was the alpha male, Molly was appropriately worshipful of me and claimed ownership of me by placing her foot on top of mine whenever possible, or slyly licking the back of my hand with a flick of her tongue when it was most unexpected. In my bad computer moments, my behavior could be described as a complete freak-out. Molly's initial reaction was to head for the door or jump onto the couch. But with the passage of time, she assumed a more take-charge role and would come to offer solace. When I'd say, "Oh shit!"—whether a shout or a whisper—Molly came running. She would place her doggie chin on my knee, her ears back, gazing soulfully up with anxious eyes as if to say, "Calm down, get a handle on it." My blood pressure would immediately normalize; I would become quiet and talk to Molly, assuring her that I was OK. And suddenly everything was OK.

When Molly finally became infirm with age and could not hold her head up, we had to put her down and bury her ashes in the backyard. I hate it that I am so damned sentimental—a grown man weeping at the loss of a dog.

Not Knowing

Things happen in small towns just like everywhere else. Except that there aren't any secrets, and the local paper is full of advertising and announcements of upcoming events, mostly good news. The bad stuff is carried by word of mouth, and to print it would be libelous because although true, it isn't supposed to be true. And besides, there's no need to print it, since everybody knows.

People in small towns of the 1940s and '50s don't talk about world-shaking events of national import. They talk about each other and the weather. The back side of this equation is that other people might know you better than you know yourself. People sometimes allow that they can do something without anyone finding out, but they never get away with it. In my father's hometown, if a crime is committed, it will be found out. But the criminal might not be prosecuted. When the safe was stolen from the high school, everybody knew Billy Gould did it. Billy wasn't such a bad kid. He just had a bit too much time on his hands. He first scandalized the community when, as an eight-year-old, with his new BB gun, he methodically and patiently shot eighty speckled martins as they perched on the large bird house atop Mr. Hornbeck's garage. Billy was the sort of boy who would catch grasshoppers in summer and gross out his playmates by slowly pulling off the grasshoppers' heads.

Later, when Bill and I were in high school together, he bragged about how he liked Black pussy, but I never

believed that any of the girls, Black or white, would want
to do it with him. Billy's dad, Fred, had operated a bar
called The Owl Club on Highway 61 about four miles north
of town at the top of the bluff overlooking Salt River. Fred
and his wife, Marie, had run the school lunch program for a
couple of years as a free-enterprise concession in an unused
room of the two-story brick school: hamburgers with
pickles, catsup, and mustard. Hot dogs sliced lengthwise
and grilled. Coke, Seven-Up, and Nehi orange soda. Plain
or chocolate milk. And Made-Rite potato ships from the
factory uptown next door to the post office.

For some reason, Fred knew how to quickly and almost
painlessly pull out a loose baby tooth. He pulled several
of mine. Once I accosted him on the street just around the
corner from McGowan's paint store. I opened my mouth to
show the loose tooth. He held my head against his side with
his left hand and forearm and carefully but firmly clasped
the tooth between the thumb and forefinger of his right
hand and pulled it right out. I think he must have done this
for quite a number of kids my age. But I don't know if he
did it for Bill. Bill always seemed to be sort of neglected.
When he grew up he became an FBI agent.

Manslaughter in our town was fairly common, murder
extremely rare. One of my grade school friends attacked his
drunken, raging father with a baseball bat. At the inquest
they called it manslaughter, as he had done it in defense
of himself and his mother. I understood. Mostly it was
old people who died, but sometimes children. Joe Griffin
drowned when I was in the second grade and he was in
the third. He had been swimming in Salt River down near

the farm-to-market road bridge. I went to his funeral at
the Baptist Church. Mrs. Croll said to me as I entered the
church, "Go on up and look at Joe, he looks so peaceful." I
walked rather self-consciously up to the casket at the front
of the church, and there was Joe resting. I guess he was
peaceful, but to me he just looked dead. I imagined that if
I had been there swimming with him, I might have saved
him. I wished I had at least been able to find the body. I
could have been some sort of hero. There were still heroes
in those days.

A few years later a boy named Shirley drowned in a
pond swimming with my friend Clarence. Folks figured
that Shirley had a heart attack or something like that.
Whenever anybody drowned, they called the Hull Rescue
Squad, and some local volunteers from over in Hull, Illinois, would come right away. They had an apparatus with
large fishhooks on it that they dragged through the water
until it snagged the drownee. Usually they found the body
within about thirty minutes. Fairly quick but too late to do
any rescuing.

Lots of people got killed in cars. And every now and
then somebody would turn over their tractor. Tom Lake
died that way. He had been Dad's partner on the farm for a
couple of years during World War II. Tom had been a good
farmer, and the partnership would have continued except
for Tom's brother Stuart, who could only speak by cussing.
He lied, cheated, and always carried a blacksnake whip.
He was relentlessly cruel and chewed tobacco. Once when
I and my then four-year-old brother were in the hayloft
watching Stuart and the Brown boys castrate some young

pigs, he yelled out that he was coming up to get us when he was through with the pigs. The screaming pigs and laughter from three full-grown men were terrible and convincing. Tom's wife, Jerry, was a Brown, and her brothers, Lewis and Tommy, sometimes worked for Tom. Folks said Tommy was a little crazy, but they said Lewis was pretty level-headed. Lewis had lost his left eye in the Philippines and was released from the Army with a glass eye, which he removed, to show me his one-eyed head with a gaping hole. I was five years old.

The '40s was a time of great seriousness. People wore suits and men wore hats and ties. People belonged to fraternal and civic organizations. My father belonged to the Masonic order, my mother, Sarah to the Eastern Star. He belonged to the Kiwanis Club, and she was a member of the Church Circle and to the rural extension club named the Laugh-a-Lot Club. They both belonged to the PTA. She was on the committee for the March of Dimes and then for many years ran the local Easter Seal campaign.

On Saturday nights, stores were open until 8:00. Farmers were in town to shop for the week. Everyone was uptown shopping and talking. If you went into the Kroger store, you could smell freshly ground coffee throughout the store. The giant coffee grinder had an urn on top that could hold five pounds. Cookies were sold from bulk containers with glass doors. You filled a bag with as many as you wanted and paid by weight. The bread was Wonder Bread wrapped in white wax paper and almost completely without substance. Dad, like most farmers, rented a meat locker in the back of the Kroger store, where the spring calf he had harvested was stored away as cuts of frozen beef wrapped in white paper.

In the summer, fundraising ice-cream socials were common. Slices of homemade cake served on a paper plate with vanilla ice cream. Folding chairs and tables set up on the vacant lot between the Shell service station and Dick Eddings' barbershop, right across Main Street from the front of the post office. People leaned on their cars talking. Children went to the movies or ran and played in the courthouse park. This town was in a certain way the center of the universe.

It's hard for me to sort out the facts or imagine them, but sometime in the middle of the 1940s, my father became ill. He had to have a gall bladder operation, and it scared the hell out of him. He sat in the backyard on a stump one afternoon and cried. He said he didn't want to die and was afraid that he was going to. My mother seemed to be disgusted by his lack of courage. She was unmoved and not compassionate. I was young and unaware. My brother and I were not included in family discussions; children were to be seen and not heard. This was said like a mantra. We were expected to do what we were told whether or not we understood the reason. We were taught not to ask questions.

Dad had his operation and had to wear a girdle for a while to hold himself together. It was in the winter, and I can still see him sitting in the living room wearing pajamas and a brown flannel housecoat. The house heated as though for an old woman, its air divested of all moisture.

Our home was cleaned on a regular schedule by my mother. Supper, the evening meal, was ready promptly at

6:30 each day. Laundry was done every Wednesday. In winter, lines were stretched in the dining room for clothes to dry on. When Dad came home for dinner, he sat in an overstuffed chair in the living room and read the paper while Mom cooked. He might say to me or to my brother, "Stop making noise or I'll thump you on the head." And to demonstrate he might thump one of us on the head, a flick of the forefinger restrained and then released by the thumb with a resounding thwack on the top of a towheaded skull.

There were curious moments of rebellion in our youthful selves in spite of what seems, in retrospect, an effort to compress the child to the flattest possible personality. It is Dad's voice booming out from his chair, "Quiet down or I'll thump you," to which my little brother responded. Sitting in the chair, Dad focuses on his reading. He hears but ignores brother Jim's clearly spoken response, "I'll thump YOU," and having stated his intention, reaches over the back of the chair to whack my preoccupied father soundly on the top of his head with a small but effective toy wooden mallet. Dad, so completely surprised and disoriented by the blow, does not strike the child. He actually thinks it a good joke on himself. I don't think I was ever so lucky.

Just one block north of the post office was the street that went east out of town and became a gravel farm-to-market road. Where this road crossed Main Street was the county courthouse on one side and on the other, the cinema, the Ralls County Records office and press, the Farm Bureau office, and, side by side, two feed stores (one the county co-op), and the Dowell and Fuqua, owned by father and son-in-law. Dowell and Fuqua was a concrete block affair with an aisle down the middle lined front to back with grain bins and piles of sacked feeds. There was a glass-enclosed office to the right of the front door and a large mill at the back. Hung high around the walls at the front were large posters depicting idealized paintings of grand champion bulls and cows of various breeds in full color. These surrounded the area where men sat to exchange small talk around a small coal oil stove.

When I was in the first grade, Darrel Fuqua was one of my friends. It was early spring, and I was riding home in the late afternoon with Dad in his blue 1940 Dodge, which preceded the grey Hudson. The Dodge had a tiny electric fan on the dash to defrost the window, and the gear shift was on the floor. The seats were of a tan fabric that was just slightly fuzzy to the touch. I sat there on the front seat and said, "Dad, why don't you buy your feeds at Roy Dowell's?"

The question was asked to obtain information. It was a child's question, looking for a clue about how things worked. Seeking reasons. Dad had been drinking. He was surrounded by his own atmosphere of whiskey-infused air.

"I'll buy my goddamned feed where I please and no smart-assed son of mine will tell me how to conduct my life. You mind you own damned business!" He shouted it at the top of his lungs, seething with rage and fury. It seemed to come out of nowhere like lightning. Searing whatever it struck with its cauterizing heat.

The Sale

There was an auction sale at the Higgenbottom place, just a half mile from our farm on Highway 19. Gilbert had built the house himself right after the war. Now he had decided to sell everything and move. We didn't know why. Some people just have to move every half-decade or so.

Auction sales are pretty big local events, kind of festive, too, with cars and pickup trucks parked along both sides of the road, like a county fair.

All the farm's possessions are set out and arranged for perusal. The tractor and tilling equipment, the mower, corn planter, manure spreader and wagon, a mélange of colors dulled with age parked side by side in a row. The milking machines and a bunch of ten-gallon milk cans are displayed on the gravel driveway beside the milk parlor. Handsaws, tools, jars of nails, two rolls of barbed wire, and other supplies are laid out next to the toolshed. The furniture on the lawn.

People move among the assembled objects touching, tapping. They greet one another. "How y'all been?" "Good to see ya." Women inspect the tables covered with knick-knacks, kitchen utensils, china. Dressers and chests stand with drawers gaping. A large armoire presides over a gathering of chairs. The smell of hot coffee is in the air, and chili. The Laugh-a-Lot women's extension club has put up the impromptu food stand. At one end is a small cattle tank of melting ice and bottled soda pop.

The ten-year-old boy I was then wanders aimlessly, feeling alone and out of place in this crowd. I see a boy of my age, Eddie, strong, big for his years. Handsome with his black curly hair. I envy curly dark hair. Never able to feel good about my straight blonde hair. Even more, I envy Eddie because everybody knows he's been driving tractors since he was six. We fought once in the third grade and I came out OK even though he kicked, which wasn't fair. Eddie walks with a bit of a swagger; he knows he is some-body. I never feel quite at ease with him, but I don't want to be alone, so I walk with him among the trucks and cars.

We wander around the outer perimeter of the parked vehicles, kicking tires and throwing clods into the pasture. The sky is a cheery blue, and there are little tufts of white fleece clouds scattered far above us. The air is still and quiet, but the clouds are moving.

I have just begun to feel comfortable with Eddie when we are joined by the Lake boys, Wayne and Dean. I've always tried to be friendly to them, because they're older. But the Lake boys seem to hate me, and I don't know why. They've taken every possible opportunity over the years to make my life miserable. Teased me mercilessly, making dirty puns and rhymes on my name. My name has always been a problem anyhow. Baylis becomes Bale Ass, and Glascock becomes Glass Pussy, or Crystal Dick, Crystal Cock. The variations are without end. Dean is the one who had called me Bale Ass and added, "You got a glass cock and a cockleburr asshole."

It seems strange to be spending time with both Eddie and the Lakes. But I am so eager for acceptance that I savor the moment, throwing caution aside. I am a child, and children are optimists. I allow that this is another day and maybe Eddie could be a friend. It will be all right. To any observer, we are four boys spending time the way boys do. Talking about the cars. Telling dirty jokes: toilet humor with sexual images.

We've been together for about fifteen minutes, long enough for me to feel relaxed, when one of the Lake boys says, "Grab him Eddie, beat him up." Right out of the blue, and it seems so senseless. I do not understand. But Eddie follows the command and grabs me around the neck in a hammerlock. My arms flail in the bright sunlight: the wings of a flightless bird. My neck cracks, and the flow of my breath is shut off by the constriction of Eddie's muscular arms.

In the distance, the sale continues. People make bids, eat apple pie, buy furniture. The Lake boys had wanted to see a fight, but it was already over. Eddie maintains his grip, then drops me like a rag.

I lie as I fell. The pain of suffocation permeates my consciousness. I can neither inhale nor exhale for seconds that feel like hours. My eyes well with silent tears of humiliation and betrayal. When I am able to breathe again, I sob convulsively.

Much later I stop crying and lie still for a long time, listening to the distant bark of the auctioneer: "Now a dollar, a dollar, I got a dollar. Now two, gimme two. Gimme two, gimme two. There's two. Now three, who'll gimme three." I can hear other voices, too, and the cawing of a crow. The sound of a car passing on the highway.

Above me the sky is blue. Rich, deep, pure, and perfect.
There is a cotton lamb playing in the clouds, and a ship.
I yearn for the luxury of those clouds. The unimaginable
softness of heaven.

It's Hard to Be an Optimist in Missouri

It's hard to be an optimist in Missouri. I have never thought of that before, but I realize how true it is. First off, there's the weather. There's just too much of it. Too hot. Too cold. Too humid. Too dry. Too wet. On and on like that. My ancestors were farmers, and weather determined the outcome of most of the life of the farmer. You had to decide way in advance of the markets what crops to put in.

Dad was driving Uncle Rec's old blue International pickup. We were bouncing along the road along the edge of the pasture. I could feel the springs in the seat, and with every slight bump the cab squeaked against the bed.

"Farming is like shooting craps," Dad said out of the blue. We were going back to look at the soybeans. "The earlier you get in your crop, the better the price. But if you plant early you might have a dry spell and the crop won't get growing, just be stunted and scrawny. Or sometimes you get a rainy spring, and you can't get the crop in until late. Your beans will mature late, and when you get to market, the price is already down. Or maybe you'll just have a dry summer and nothing will grow.

"Back in the summer of 1935, it was so dry we had no grass in the pasture. We fed the milk cows straw with molasses poured on it. The stickiest damned mess you ever saw. And the flies! You just wouldn't believe it. Somehow we got through. You don't really have a choice."

I'd heard about the molasses before. Maybe Dad was trying to tell me that I shouldn't think of going into farming. But if that was the case, why was I working on the farm and why I was taking vocational agriculture? It was because I didn't really have a choice. The New London High School curriculum featured Vocational Ag because most of the students came from farms and expected to become farmers.

I knew I wasn't going to be a farmer and had known that since I was six years old. It had come out in a conversation with Gladys Kruger, Felix Jewell's (aka Peally's) live-in housekeeper. I had walked up the highway to visit her one day after school. We were in the living room looking out across the highway at a field of corn and just chatting. She was nice to talk to because she seemed to take me seriously, like I was a real person, not just a little boy. And I was momentarily speculating about what I might be when I grew up.

Musician was one possibility. Or maybe a doctor. But I didn't say farmer. Just the same, living on a farm meant you would practice farming. But still, I did get to study music after a fashion. I had begun taking piano lessons in the first grade but always wanted to play the trumpet. And it was about the time I was in the sixth grade when the school hired a music teacher and I got my first horn. A man came to the school one night and sold trumpets and clarinets and trombones. Never mind that no one knew how to play. And how could we know that Henry McClintock, the man hired to be the music teacher, was hopelessly incompetent? The high school boys called him a pansy, even though he was a prodigious breeder, with three little kids and a fourth on the way. But Mr. McClintock was somewhat effeminate. We took what we got in New London. So I got a little music and a lot of farming.

The high school Vocational Ag classes were not all that memorable. I did learn that the reason the pigs will eat fresh cow shit is that there is leftover nutrition in the manure that pigs can use. It's called the animal protein factor. The teacher was a man named Merle Wenniker. He was married to a beautiful blond woman and had two little daughters. He had a good sense of humor, and the students liked him. The whole class came out to our farm one morning to learn how to castrate pigs. We had a sow with nine three-week-old piglets, perfect subjects. We were all in the pen in the red barn behind our house.

Little pigs do protest when you hold them, and they squeal even louder when you cut them. That's what Dad had always called castrating an animal, as in "We'll cut the pigs on Friday."

Dad always carried a pocketknife with the short blade very sharp for cutting pigs. The Ag class was halfway through castrating the second pig when the sow came charging in. We had forgotten to close the gate. A three-hundred-pound sow about to defend her squealing baby is not to be trifled with. All my classmates discovered they could leap over a much taller fence than they had previously imagined. I was holding the pig and was much slower to respond. I held the pig out to the sow as a shield. Somehow I exited, abandoning the partially castrated piglet, which had a dangling nut. I was shaken but unscathed.

I had gone to Future Farmers of America camp the summer before I was to actually be a freshman. We rode the yellow school bus, singing "Ninety-nine bottles of beer on the wall" most of the way to Lake of the Ozarks. Merle drove. There was much joking about my obligation as the newest FFA member, and the youngest, to spend the night in "the barrel." The mythical barrel had a knothole in the side into which various persons would insert their penis to receive a blowjob from the occupant. I did find this funny. When we got to our cabin, I was subjected to a ritual hazing, which consisted of getting my pants pulled off and my pubic region doused with Old Spice shaving lotion. I smarted for quite a while from both the stinging alcohol and the humiliation.

Because I was adept with words, I was assigned to participate in a discussion group. Merle had suggested several things I would be able to mention as things our FFA chapter had done for fund-raising. I must have made up some stuff, because I got a little gold medal with the FFA symbol as the best discusser in the camp that summer.

I also took the junior lifesaving class. At the end of the week, I had to swim one hundred yards out to a canoe and back to shore, pass some kind of written test, and jump from the dock into the lake and save the instructor as he faked drowning. I weighted about a hundred and ten pounds at the time; the instructor was a couple of inches taller and outweighed me by fifty pounds.

Swimming mightily, I valiantly took hold of the drown-ing instructor. Actually, those who saw the test said that as

I reached the instructor, he grabbed my head and pushed me under. As taught in the preceding three days, as I was completely underwater, I grabbed the flailing instructor at the waist and turned him, placing myself behind him. Then I surfaced behind him, somehow maintaining a hold, reached over his shoulder and across his chest with my right arm, placing my hand in his armpit. Then with my free arm I swam madly toward the shore using a one-armed sidestroke, dragged him up onto the beach, and administered the chest pressure resuscitation practiced in 1955. The instructor awarded me a Red Cross Junior Life Saving certificate even though I forgot to remove the nose clips he wore while drowning.

On the final evening of camp there was a vesper service on the shore at sunset. I had been asked to bring my horn to camp in anticipation of the ceremony. The swimming instructor ferried me across the lake almost to the far shore in a canoe. It was quiet and beautiful. The lake was as smooth as a mirror. At the appropriate moment on a signal from a flashlight, I began to play taps. It was at this moment that someone crossed the lake in a speedboat. It sort of broke the spell.

There had been a dance on Wednesday night with a busload of Girl Scouts imported from a camp nearby. I mustered the courage to ask a girl to dance and was refused. The whole week seemed to be fraught with peril and frustration. I felt that I was in the wrong place, with no one I could really think of as a friend. If loneliness, frustration, and humiliation were character building, the camp must have been successful in my case. But I think that is

how I felt about each of my various camp experiences—
except for music camp.

It must have been that summer that I went to Egyptian
Music Camp on a scholarship given to me by the New
London Women's Club. The camp took place in southern
Illinois on the grounds of a racetrack. The dorms were
bunkbeds placed under the stadium. I actually found people
I enjoyed being with. There was one afternoon in particular that seemed wonderful. I sat with several older guys
on the bunks listening to an LP of opera overtures. The
music from a tiny speaker in a portable record player was
thrilling. I hungered for this music. Nothing like this could
be heard on the radio, and I didn't have a record player.
I seemed to be accepted among this small group. One
of them was named Eddie Ghent, who played a trumpet
solo during the final night's concert. We corresponded for
several years after. He was two grades ahead of me and
went to Southern Illinois University. I later learned that
Harry Partch and Buckminster Fuller each had taught there,
so it must have been a special place.

During that year of school I had one friend, a person I
had known for a couple of years named Herman Dodd.
Herman's dad ran a junkyard in Hannibal, a place
surrounded by the carcasses of crashed automobiles and
scrap metal of all kinds. We were an odd pair. I was interested in classical music and wanted to build a hi-fi. He
was interested in cars, cars, cars. And girls. We were both
interested in girls but both alone in the world. I went roller
skating with Herman. We thought we might meet a girl at
the rink but didn't. I didn't drive yet. Herman had a couple

of dates with one of the New London girls, but that didn't work out.

Herman never made very good grades. Academic stuff didn't interest him. But he knew the displacement of just about any engine you could name and the firing order of the spark plugs. Could dismantle and rebuild any engine. He absorbed that kind of information without knowing that he was learning. He would tell me about the Offies—racecars with Offenhouser engines. And the Cummings diesel engines that were used in racing cars. And he would make the doppler sound of a race car roaring by. He loved the Indy 500 and stock car racing. He lived and breathed cars and engines.

Then one of the teachers said something to Herman that hurt his sense of dignity.

"You are either dumb or lazy," she had said when he didn't turn in an assignment. He said he wouldn't take that from anybody. There were tears in his eyes as he was leaving. I stood with him in the hallway and begged him to stay in school. There were tears in my eyes, too. It hurt me to see him go. And I thought, too, that he was making a mistake not finishing high school. But Herman probably knew the things he needed to make his way in life. He would be a mechanic and deal in used cars and have a good life on his own terms. He left the school and my life. We were never in touch after that day.

That was the year I got sick. I had been asked to play a trumpet solo at a special evening planned by the county health nurse at the Center school auditorium. By then I was taking lessons weekly in Hannibal from Bob Dillinger, a sophomore music major at Kirksville State Teachers College. I had agreed to play, but on the evening of the event, I didn't feel well. When the moment came for me to perform, I felt too bad to play and said that I just couldn't do it. The nurse who had organized the occasion was really angry.

The next morning I didn't wake up at the usual time. I felt even worse than the night before, so my brother Jim had to milk the cow while I slept in. By noon I was still in bed, groggy, limbs laden. I could barely move. Mom decided that I should visit Dr. Landau. I walked out the front door to the car with the slowness of a zombie, my strides short and deliberate. My head ached. As I sat on the examining room table, the doctor took my temperature, whacked my knees with a rubber mallet, looked into my eyes and mouth.

"Sarah," he said to Mom. "We have to take him to the hospital right now. This is rheumatic fever."

I was in the hospital for two weeks. The county health nurse told Mom she felt really bad about being mad at me for not playing the solo. This was the first vacation I had had in a long time. Nothing to do but lie in bed. I didn't hurt, I just had to stay in bed, not walk or do anything stressful. St. Elizabeth's was the Catholic hospital where I had been born on a hot summer night fifteen years earlier.

I was awakened in the middle of each night to receive a cortisone shot. I was lonely enough that I tried to engage in conversation with the nun, but she said she had too much to do. Each afternoon the priest, Father Pack, would drop by to say hello. He joked about the nuns. Said they were so isolated from ordinary life that they didn't know the price of a can of beans. He said one of the nuns had to have some surgery on her leg, and the surgeon asked the good sister about the calluses on her knees. "I do pray," she responded. He thought that was pretty funny, and I did too.

During the second week I read *Lust for Life*, a novel about Van Gogh. It was full of words I couldn't pronounce, like the brother's name, Theo. There was a short scene of erotic fantasy in the story that coincided with my arrival at puberty, and while reading it I had my first conscious ejaculation, which felt great and left me with an embarrassing mess on my pajamas. For the next couple of months, I put some considerable effort into re-creating that experience.

Uncle Rec

In the family legend it is Uncle Rec who walked barefooted in the snow. A bachelor all his life, he seemed already an old man when I was a child. He shook with a palsy that modulated his voice, making it difficult for me to understand his speech. Modest of height, slender, sinewy, and tough. When he was a young man, the muscles on his arms bulged like baseballs. In summer he wore a straw hat and a felt one in winter.

His name was Rector, but everyone called him Rec or Rex. Granddad's youngest brother, he was my great-uncle. There were three brothers, each of whom took a third of the original family farm. Uncle Rec's farm, the middle parcel of the three, lay on the north side of Highway 19 about two miles west of New London, adjacent to Granddad's farm. A gravel road snakes diagonally from the highway across the front pasture to the row of trees referred to as the railroad track. We still speak of the railroad track as if it were there, even though the iron rails were taken out in the mid-1930s.

The gravel road crosses the roadbed of old short-line track and leads past the house where Uncle Rec and Granddad were born. A big white house, two stories, with a dinner bell out back. A bisecting hallway from the front door to the kitchen had pegs on the wall for hanging coats and hats. Outside, clapboard siding. A wide porch across the front for sitting on Sundays. I visited the house after it had been empty for half a dozen years. A large table in one of the side rooms had been used for sugar-curing hams. The room still smelled strongly of the ham sweetness. From the house it was only a hundred and fifty yards to the horse barn, a large red structure with granaries, a large hayloft above the middle. And still farther to the dairy barn with its two silos, its concrete milking parlor. It is land at the edge of the prairie, land with fields that rise gently and then slope toward woods of oak and black walnut, sycamore and elm, mulberry, dogwood, hedge, and locust.

From around 1905 through the '20s, Uncle Rec made a weekly trip to Hannibal delivering live and dressed chickens. And if he had shot any, dressed rabbits, sometimes as many as fifty. And two hundred pounds of butter. Butter that had to be churned on Wednesday and hand wrapped. Grandma and Granddad and Dad, as a little boy, all worked with Uncle Rec on Wednesday nights kneading salt into the butter, pressing it into the forms, wrapping it. Placing the one-pound cubes of butter in the large icebox to be cooled by three hundred pounds of ice. Uncle Rec churned the butter in the backyard using a fifty-gallon wooden barrel turned by a small two-cycle gas engine. It was necessary to stop the rig every five minutes to release gas pressure created as the butter began to form. One hot summer day, Uncle Rec went to sleep, and the neglected churn exploded, throwing butter all over the house, even on the roof. It was a dry summer, and the smell of rancid butter lingered until the house was cleansed by fall rains.

Uncle Rec had a route of residential customers for butter and eggs, chickens, and the dressed rabbits. He also sold to a grocery store. Those deliveries had been made by horse and wagon and later with a Model-T Ford modified into a kind of delivery van.

By the time I knew Uncle Rec, he was driving an old rust-colored International pickup truck. I rode in the back of it once, all the way to Quincy, sitting on a load of sacked soybeans. There was a mill in Quincy that ground soybeans and made them smell wonderful, like fresh coffee, only sweeter. Mom rode in the front with Uncle Rec and said she was scared all the way because Uncle Rec's shotgun was lying at an angle from the floor up against the back window. I was in the truck bed, right where it was pointed.

Uncle Rec always had a shotgun in that truck, and he kept it loaded. Whenever he saw a rabbit or a squirrel, he stopped and shot it, picked up his dead game, and threw it into the back of the truck. Dad said he was a hell of a good shot but only hunted for the game, not for sport. I remember at least one time when Uncle Rec forgot to give the dead rabbits to Grandma and they just lay in the back of that rusty pickup rotting. The smell didn't seem to bother him.

Once in a while he would get a nosebleed. Probably picked his nose. He'd stop it by stuffing a piece of white bread up the bleeding nostril, which stuck out and became tinged with red where the bread met his nose. At Christmas he always gave gifts of money to the children: my brothers and cousins—a dollar, or maybe two each. I always hoped for more, but it never happened.

Uncle Rec was a good judge of animals; pigs, cows, horses. He never knew exactly how many pigs he had but could tell if one was missing. You could visit the farm,

and only a few hogs would be visible, but when Uncle
Rec called the hogs, they seemed to come from everywhere, from under every building, wagon, and fence, from
all directions until you were surrounded by a sea of pigs.
Most farmers castrated hogs at about forty pounds, but
Uncle Rec sometime didn't cut them until they weighed
well over a hundred pounds. Catching and holding down
a one-hundred-pound pig while someone cuts off his balls
is hard and dirty work. But the reward is a feast of fried
Rocky Mountain oysters, Uncle Rec's favorite food.

Uncle Rec didn't have much of a program for shipping
mature hogs to market. When he needed money, he shipped
hogs. Sometimes they were monstrous. During World
War II, hog prices were high, and Uncle Rec made a lot of
money. His fences were always in bad repair, and he was
forever having to pay someone for part of a field of corn or
beans that his hogs had eaten.

When I was about nine years old, I went to the Hannibal
Auction Barn with Uncle Rec. I got bored after a while
looking at the cows and calves. They all looked about the
same to me. But Uncle Rec loved looking at the animals,
watching the people. The bark of the auctioneer was music
to his ears, like the chant of a bard. It was an autumn day,
and I went outside where an old Indian was selling oil
and salve made from rattlesnakes. The Indian said he had
some rattlesnakes in the trunk of his car. I begged to see
them, but he said he couldn't open the trunk because the
snakes were having babies. Uncle Rec came out at the end
of the sale and listened to the Indian's spiel but didn't buy
anything. Said he didn't believe there were any snakes in

the Indian's trunk. Didn't think the salve would remove warts, either.

In the era before tractors, Uncle Rec raised mules.

"He was real good with mules," Dad said. "Knew how to work with 'em. The more ornery and mean they were, the more he seemed to like it. He had a favorite. A white mule named Jenny. Now that mule knew how to open a gate. If a gate was held closed by a sliding board or a chain, that mule could open it. You had to use number nine wire and twist it good to keep that mule in."

For some reason, Uncle Rec's horses and mules liked to bite, and you always had to be paying attention about that. He raised and sold lots of mules over the years.

Uncle Rec owned a team of large sorrel draft mares with white faces. One morning, I woke to find the two giants lying beside the highway near our front yard. The mares had gotten out during the night and onto the highway. A drunk driver in a green Pontiac had hit them. Destroyed the man's car, which came to rest in the middle of our front pasture. One mare lay with its legs straight out from its body, like a toppled statue.

There was about Uncle Rec an almost casual attitude toward death and danger. He had often been seen to walk up to and pet his Jersey bull, a beast that had treed a hired hand who had dared to walk in the same pasture. Uncle Rec had to lead the bull away so the man could come down.

At the back of the dairy barn were two silos about nine feet apart. Uncle Rec had been known to jump from the top of one to the other some thirty-five feet up.

Early evenings in the summer, he would park his International pickup in front of Mae Reilley's house, across the street from the Christian Church. If you drove by you would see him sitting there on the porch with Mae drinking lemonade or iced tea. Maybe having a piece of cake. Mae did most of the talking. As a young man, Uncle Rec had been deeply in love with a bright and beautiful woman who chose to marry an older, more prosperous man named Owens. Uncle Rec never quite got over it.

Over the years he was given to periods of deep depression and would stay in bed for days or even weeks, leaving day-to-day running of the farm to the hired hand. The summer of 1940, before Dad started work at the post office, Uncle Rec had one of his down times. The hired hand had quit. It fell to Dad, newly married to Mom, to milk Uncle Rec's cows. Twice each day Dad fed and milked his own cows, then Mom cleaned the equipment and the milk parlor while Dad went to milk Uncle Rec's herd. That summer it was impossible to hire help, so Mom and Dad had to put up the hay for both farms, too.

Uncle Rec could snap out of these moods as quickly as they came upon him, and suddenly he would put his hat on and be off to a sale or back at work on the farm as though nothing had happened. In his bedroom he kept a stash of Milky Way candy bars for those times when he didn't want to come out. Sometimes he would shit in his wastebasket.

In the years that I knew him, he lived in town with Granddad and Grandma. He had his own room off the enclosed back porch. A simple room with a bed and a secretary, a lamp and a single chair. I remember his room as having a strong smell, the dried sweat of an old man. He asked me to come in one day, said he had something for me. A gold ring with our common initials and two pairs of gold-plated initialed cufflinks of an antique style that had a fixed post. One of the pairs had an oval shape with tiny stipples around the perimeter. I liked that pair. The ring's details had been smoothed away with wear, all except the incised initial. The metal had become quite thin.

In 1952, Uncle Rec went into an extended depression, which lasted for two years. For some reason Dad was reluctant to get involved. So Uncle Tubby, the husband of Dad's sister, took over management of the farm. He spent money fixing up the road in from the highway. He bought a new grinder and a giant feed mixer. He bought a new tractor and built a new milking parlor. Got new milking equipment. Uncle Tubby didn't know the first thing about farming and did not seek advice from people who did. He had been raised in town and had never lived for a single day on a farm. At the end of the two years, Uncle Rec's cash reserves had been depleted and the farm brought to insolvency. Dad finally had to take over. He closed down the dairy, sold the herd and equipment at auction, and gradually got the farm back to solvency.

Uncle Rec rebounded more slowly this time. Most of the fields were leased out. The animals were gone except for a few beef calves. Uncle Rec still drove an International pickup, a blue one. He came and went from the farm to town. The shotgun had been put away.

Uncle Rec had been a practical man of simple tastes. He used to point out the beautiful barns that one could see here and there along the highway on a trip to St. Louis. He said those farms with good-looking barns belonged to people who didn't farm for a living.

There were a lot of mysteries in my family. Things we didn't talk about, didn't ask about, didn't even know about. A lot about Uncle Rec was in this realm. Most of the dark things I know about my family I learned from my mother. There is about her the quality of an imp, and she tells me things that open my eyes and startle me. It was one of my questions about Dad that prompted Mom to open the dark secrets about Uncle Rec.

"Why's Dad always so depressed?" I said to Mom one day, thinking of Dad sitting with his white hair gazing out the window, an expression of wistful sadness on his face. This is Dad's default condition.

Mom said, "Your dad's probably thinking about his mother and Uncle Rec. As a little boy he saw them together." And then Mom told me it was Finn Peoples who told her about Uncle Rec and Grandma.

Finn said, "All the colored peoples knowed about it. White folks didn't bother to hide things from us coloreds. Cause the colored peoples is just plain invisible when they's working for you. Rec lived right there in that house with Steve and Mary from the time they was married on. That ain't so hard to figure out."

It doesn't seem right to ask Dad whether he did or didn't see them. But I did ask questions about Uncle Rec. "What did he do?" and "What was he like?" and Dad couldn't quite find words to describe him. It was the pauses between his words, the awkwardness as he searched to find the right word.

"He was a pistol, a spade, he was a renegade," Dad said, and he thought about it for ten or fifteen seconds. "He was really something else."

There is a picture of Uncle Rec as a young man in a suit. Handsome with a jaunty rake to his hat. Granddad's image is more sober, staid: a good and Christian man. Honest, upright, devout. Grandma was a high-strung and demanding woman who always got what she wanted. Maybe she had needs that Granddad didn't take care of, so she turned to Uncle Rec.

"Why else," said Mom, "did Grandma have Uncle Rec live with them all those years? Cook his meals. Mend his clothes. Take better care of him than she did of Granddad."

I visit the cemetery with Mom, looking at the family grave markers, the dates. I have difficulty placing most of the names on the stones, and Mom is prompting me. The whole family that preceded us is there. Great-grandparents, uncles, aunts, cousins. Granddad and Grandma, Uncle Tubby, Uncle Rec. I am surprised to notice that Uncle Rec died on my birthday in 1963. I had forgotten.

It is a warm summer day, a Missouri summer day. Humid. Fat clouds starting to look like rain. Here, away from my everyday life, I feel that I am in a place apart from time. These stones laid out in rows. The grass under my feet. The curved, cloud-laden sky moves above. Gnats buzz in my face. My mother, in consort and concert with God, has given me life. Mom, the maker of things. Sewing and cooking, painting the house or a canvas. The curious one, the one who wanted to know, the one who took me to the museums, the concerts. The one with the piercing brown eyes, head cocked just so, with her own little smugness. The one who taught me compassion and love but refused to help me tie my shoes. Gave me the clues that sex was dark and unspeakable. Then spoke about it. Mom, the trickster.

And we are standing together in the midst of my ancestors' bones. A gnat has gotten into my eye, and I hear them buzzing in my ear. My mother's voice. The voice of comfort and solace. A voice that has turned me on a dime and sent me tumbling into fresh orbits. Mom the imp. And her voice says to me:

"Likelihood is, Uncle Rec is your grandfather."

Mom: Of the Earth, Above the Earth

"I was eight years old when I got red bloomers for Christmas, and I was so proud of them I wanted to trip and fall down so everyone could see my bright red undies."

It is a story she told me when I was eight. I have a picture of Mom at about the time she graduated from high school. Her hair is in flat curls close to her face. Her eyes are piercingly intelligent, and her smile is knowing. She is beautiful in the way that all women are, in the full blossom of youth, but also in a timeless way. I think she might have dated my father only a matter of weeks before they were married on New Year's eve in 1939 in the living room of the justice of the peace. Almost impromptu, no church, no relatives, no reception. It's hard to say how the proposal came about. I think they were in love.

This, the mom who seemed to have a complete balance between dark and light, ever critical of her husband, member of her church, her clubs, her community. Yet full of compassion for their sufferings, their mistakes, their problems. The phone call came early one afternoon. Her friend Mary McGowan was in the hospital.

"They operated," Mom said. "They cut her open and she was full of cancer. There was nothing they could do. They just sewed her back up." And Mom started to cry. I didn't see Mom cry very often. Sometimes she would cry in desperation: "I just don't know what makes Edward drink." And she would cry. "I can't understand. I just can't understand."

I made her cry once when we were in St. Louis. I had brought along a high school friend and wanted to go off and be away from Mom.

"Mom," I said, "we want to go off and goof around. You're cramping our style." And she started to cry. I had hurt her feelings. I was joking in the way she had taught me to joke. I apologized, and we stayed with her that afternoon.

From her I learned to criticize others, make judgments. I said of a third grader, "Merl White is a jerk, I hate him. He's a bully." Mom would say, "Well, he may seem like all of those things, but his mother loves him." As though no matter how bad you were, your mother's love was unconditional. And no matter who you were, there was someone who saw you in a favorable light.

It was Mom whose love was the foundation of my being, who was also the source of the most unsettling information. Information that could, in the flash of a second, literally transform the flat Earth upon which I stood. Euclidean parallel lines receding to infinity, a dynamic universe of spheres, motion, of light, darkness, good, and evil. And the realm of people of revolution. A world of revolutionary ideas.

It was a specific moment in the cornfield behind the white dairy barn at about 8:40 a.m. We were walking north toward the railroad tracks and the woods. The morning sun was on our backs, and the full moon was still high in the sky. A cloudless blue sky. And Mom says to me, the six-year-old boy walking beside her, "You see the moon

137

right there. It's a round ball out in space. Two hundred and forty thousand miles from the Earth. It travels in a circle around the Earth. The Earth is round like a ball. Eight thousand miles right through the middle. And the Earth travels in a circle around the sun." She went on without prompting. We had never broached these ideas before. I had never heard them discussed before.

"The Sun is a star just like the stars we see at night. But the Sun is much closer." I felt cut loose from my moorings. I was floating in space. Where was I going? How was I going to stay attached to the Earth in the face of this startling new information? And then, before I caught my breath, as if one idea was attached to the other, she told me about people who live in Russia.

"They're communists and they have no freedom and they have no property. They can't own anything. Everything is owned by the state. And they're not permitted to worship God." This all sounded ominous and terrible.

"What did they do on Sunday?" I asked. I was barefooted, and the field was full of the stubble of harvested corn.

When I was six years old, my task each day after school was to carry a small bucket to the dairy barn to get milk for the table. I would dunk a metal cup into the ten-gallon can and fill the tiny bucket. I would drink a cup of the fresh, warm milk, the temperature of my own body, foamy and delicious. One day I went into the milking parlor to watch the hired hand. He instructed me:

"When you get home, pull a hair out of your head and ask your mom if it is one of her cunt hairs." Thinking this to be good sport, I did. The painful, humiliating switching. Bare bottom. Peach branch. A new rule: you couldn't say "cunt."

I was about eight when we were in the J.C. Penny's store in Hannibal. A woman was wearing a fur coat, and I was standing close to her so I could touch the fur. Mom made me come away from the fur lady. I walked up to the pyramidal display of Kotex boxes and said, "Mom, what's Kotex?" She shushed me smartly and whispered that she would tell me later.

That evening as we waited in the Hudson while Dad went into the liquor store, I asked again.

"Mom, you said you'd tell me what Kotex is." It was difficult for her to talk about, that much was clear. I could make no sense of it all except that a woman's body produces some kind of something. And you didn't talk about it. Because it was dirty and awful.

I was fifteen when Mom was pregnant with her fifth child. I was embarrassed at the very idea that my parents did the thing that made people pregnant. It was too disgusting to even think about. The summer was hot, and Mom, extended tummy and all, helped me and Carl Tischer unload a wagon full of hay at our barn. Carl seemed to be having heart palpitations from the heat and was breathing hard, sweating profusely. Nothing could stop Mom, forty and pregnant, or slow her down.

I was cultivating corn one afternoon that same summer, and Mom was driving home from town. She parked her car off the highway and started to climb the fence. Bringing me a coke, having difficulty climbing the fence with that distended body. She began to laugh at the absurdity of herself trying to climb the fence. "Oh, fuck," she said. And laughed some more.

Then she told me a joke.

"A man comes home from work to find his wife preparing a meal for the preacher. 'Fuck the preacher,' the man says. 'I did fuck the preacher,' says the wife. Now he's hungry.' " Mom saying "fuck" sent me reeling. I thought I knew her. I thought I knew the rules. It's almost as if she had decided I was too prudish and needed to loosen me up a bit.

The baby was born a month later during the week of the fall street fair in Hannibal, where I played in a small ensemble from the Hannibal High band that accompanied the highwire and trampoline act that was entertaining the crowds. The baby was a girl. Mom had wanted me to be a girl, sometimes putting a bow in my hair. Named after her mother, Netty, the infant was perfect, she said. A beautiful little face. The nurse had brought the baby for Mom to see. The baby's crown was wrapped in gauze and covered with a white cloth. There was no skull above the forehead. The brain was completely unprotected. Nettie lived only a few days. Mom, in spite of her grief, had arranged for the eye bank in St. Louis to receive Netty's eyes. A highway patrolman came to the hospital and drove the organs to their destination. Mom would extract some small victory from the ashes of her grief.

On the occasion of a family reunion when I had adult children of my own, I rode through town with Mom and my brother John. I operated a video camera, and John, in the back seat, controlled the recorder. We photographed Mom as she drove past houses we had known. Things vaguely familiar yet made strange by the passage of time.

Mom says, "Is that thing on?" and John says "no," hoping to get a genuine candid moment. So Mom continues.

"You know, your Aunt Lucy has a new boyfriend. And I sure hope he doesn't come today, 'cause I just hate the son of a bitch."

I thought it was a fine and humorous moment. And it would have been, but John proceeded to show the tape at the family gathering. When Mom's line hit the screen, the family scattered, sent spinning by Mom's rhetoric. Her sister Sue said, "Well, I'm not leaving, I want to hear what she says about me." Aunt Lucy and her children and her boyfriend were all out boating at the time. I was disappointed that John erased the tape. Mom had been caught in the act but seemed not to have significant regrets. I think she experienced a cleansing freedom in giving voice to her dark thoughts. A bit like the little joke she made a day later when we are videotaping a family oral history. Mom and Dad were sitting on the front porch swing.

"He thinks you're his kids, but he don't know for sure, and I'm gonna keep him guessing." She laughs heartily, knowing in her heart that she has played the ultimate trick on all of us, deciding whose genes we've inherited.

In her retirement years she takes pride in the simplicity of her life. You can't buy her a gift because she has everything she wants or needs. Still, she never passes up a yard sale. "I got everything I have on except my underwear for less than two dollars. This pair of shoes was fifty cents. This blouse was a quarter. The belt was a quarter. And this skirt cost fifty cents." The only extravagance permitted: breakfast out every morning. And a New Buick every third year. But the car is Dad's doing.

Imp and trickster that my mother is and was, she insisted that we children go to Sunday school every week unless bedridden. And she operated on the assumption that we never told her anything other than the truth. She had a certain kind of faith in her offspring. In their inherent goodness. In their absolute honesty. And she thought schooling was a good thing. Piano lessons. College. For a brief time, while my half-brother, Steve, lived in Chicago, he studied a curious medical discipline called naturopathy. Mom thought it sounded like some kind of quackery.

"It's a good thing to be in school, even if you're learning to be a criminal," she said.

I guess it really boils down to the fact that Mom has a lot of anger in her. She said recently, observing that I have come to prefer my coffee warm, "He likes his coffee and his women lukewarm." In front of my wife. My wife lukewarm? What does she mean? We haven't decided. Mom wants to keep me off balance.

"Wherever you go," Mom said, "there will always be the moon and the stars. You can leave Missouri, but you will always come back." And then, with a smile and loving mockery in her voice: "You can leave me, but you will always be in my heart. When you get to California, get a haircut."

The History Lesson

"Your grandmother was in the DAR. That means she could trace her family all the way back to the Revolutionary War. That's on the Hayes side of the family. Your granddad was never interested in that kind of thing."

Dad said this at breakfast one morning. He wasn't usually home for breakfast unless it was a national holiday. So it must have been Armistice Day or Columbus Day. Somehow the conversation had wandered into family history, which always seemed to interest Dad. He was in a good mood, which was unusual. He wasn't the least bit sullen.

"Now this farm was purchased in 1875 by your great-grandfather. He had three sons—your granddad Steven Clay, your Uncle Rector Baylis, and your Uncle Jimmy Green. Each of the sons got one third of the land. Uncle Jimmy Green died in his forties. He'd built that house up the road where the Logans live. That farm had been his. And the house was a prefabricated house from Sears Roebuck. They delivered it with everything precut and ready to assemble. Put that thing up in about a week."

Dad got up from the table and went to his bedroom and returned with several items we hadn't seen. He laid them out on the table. There was a muzzle-loading pistol, a pair of rusted handcuffs, and a folded yellow leather thing with ties.

"Your great-grandfather made the money to buy this farmland by driving his own mule team and wagonloads of merchandise from Missouri to the West before the intercontinental rail line was completed. It was hard work and dangerous. Started during the California Gold Rush. Carried his earnings back in this money belt. Look, here you can see the impressions of the gold coins."

Dad unfolded the yellow leather. It was long enough to go around a thick man's belly and deep enough to hold a lot of coins. There were rounded bulges on the surface. I touched it to feel the bulges. It was neither soft nor hard. Sort of in between.

"Those mules were tough, and it took a strong man to work them. Anyway, mules are sure-footed and ideal on rough roads or steep grades. And they can handle the heat better than draft horses. That's why there are so many of them here in Missouri. They're really good work animals, if you understand them. Your grandfather did. Bred and raised there right here on this farm, sold them. People thought they were ornery. But if you got to know them, they could do a lot of work."

Dad picked up the pair of handcuffs. The heavy iron cuffs had rusted solid, although the connecting chain links were still loose.

"During the Civil War, your Great Uncle Absalom Grimes was a spy for the Confederate army. He had been a riverboat pilot on the Mississippi. When the war broke out, he was in St. Louis and he was brought into the office of the local Union commander, along with two other pilots. The three men were going to be conscripted into the Union army as pilots. The officer told the men to wait in his office until he returned. All three took the opportunity to escape and thus avoided serving in the Union army. Your great-uncle's sympathies were with the Confederate side. This area around here was a slave-holding region. That's why you see so many colored people here. They are the grandchildren and great-grandchildren of slaves.

"Absalom Grimes knew the river, so he could easily travel downstream floating on broken tree limbs to go past enemy lines. He carried correspondence from mothers and girlfriends to Confederate soldiers and returned with letters from the soldiers. He was caught several times. Each time sentenced to death by firing squad and escaped. On one occasion he was held in a room wearing these very hand-cuffs, awaiting execution at sunrise. He managed to woo a young woman in the next room with sweet conversation. He persuaded her to pull a string threaded under the door to keep the chair in his room rocking. It happened that your great-uncle had very flexible hands and could easily slip handcuffs off. The guard posted outside heard the chair rockin' all night and assumed that his prisoner would be there in the morning. He seemed to have nine lives. Here are the handcuffs from that particular escape."

I looked at the money belt and the handcuffs. I couldn't see how these stories could be real. My life seemed so ordinary.

"What about the pistol, Dad?"

"Well, nobody seems to know where that comes from. But it certainly is old. So there must be some history there."

The funny thing about all this history is that my brother Jim and I never discussed it. And I never told anyone else about having a Confederate spy in the family. Then, in

1953, an article about my great-uncle Absalom Grimes appeared in the Sunday magazine section of the *St. Louis Post-Dispatch*. It was all there. Everything Dad had said. Except Dad hadn't known that one of the three river pilots had been Samuel Clemens. When I saw Buster Keaton's wonderful movie *The General*, the scene of the prisoner escaping while the girl in the next room moved the rocking chair with a string was in there. It made me wonder: which came first, the family story Dad could tell, or the one Buster Keaton told?

Everybody Knowed

In a small town like New London, there weren't many secrets. About the time I was in the first grade, the telephone was an oak box attached to the wall. The box had a crank on the side, which you turned when you wanted to get the operator. You talked into a kind of horn-shaped thing that stuck out sort of like the nose on a face, right under the two bells that stared bug-eyed into the room. When the phone rang a long ring and two shorts, that was for us, and Mom would put the earpiece to her head and say "hello" into the thing that stuck out in front. When you called someone, you could say the number, "three two six," or you could say, "Merle, give me Dee Ann, would you?" Merle Conn was the operator, or it might be Marlyn Odessa. Most everybody knew the telephone operators, and the operators knew who called who and what they were likely to be calling about.

Everybody had a party line, usually three or four on the same one. Maybe even five or six families shared a line. You could have a private line, like Dr. Bonnell. But most people didn't. So if you wanted to make a call, you'd first pick up the handset and listen to find out if the line was free. Margaret Logan on up the road, or Sophie Katzenberg even farther, might already be using the line, and you'd have to wait until they finished talking. Sometimes a phone conversation might go on for quite a while.

"Well, I reckon so, at least that's what I heard. (pause) Don't that just beat everything. I can't imagine what the girl was thinking . . ."

Sometimes you'd have to have to wait half an hour for the line to be free. Or you'd make a call and as you're talking, you hear a click on the line. Someone has just picked up to see if the line is free. But then there's no second click, which means that instead of hanging up, your neighbor is listening in on your conversation. And of course, Merle or Thelma at the switchboard listened in whenever there weren't any other calls being placed. There just weren't many secrets in New London.

Everybody knew when Johnny Newlan's stepsister was sleeping with him, because the woman who came to do laundry each week found hairpins in his sheets. The cleaning lady didn't tell everybody, but if she told two people, and each of them told two people, then it was only a matter of time until if you told somebody, they'd say, "Isn't that just shocking?" Or, "Oh, that's old news, I heard that last week."

The phone company was owned by my cousin Richard Glascock. Richard was about the same age as Dad. They went to school together. According to Dad, Richard owned lots of AT&T stock. Had gone to Annapolis. But in a small town, most everybody dressed the same. And Richard was a tightwad, wouldn't spend a dime if he didn't have to.

When television arrived in the fifties, Cousin Richard sold television sets. And you knew who had a TV, because if you had a TV, you had to have the antenna on a tall pole with a rotor to turn the antenna toward the station you wanted to watch. We were kind of late getting one.

Anyway, Cousin Richard made a good deal of money selling TVs, mostly right out of his house. One day when we brought a farmer into his living room to look at a television, Richard had mud on his boots and tracked it across the floor. His wife entered the room in a state of rage, yelling, "I just scrubbed and waxed these floors, and look what you've done!" And with that, she reached down, grabbed the small throw rug he was standing on, and pulled it from under him, dumping him flat on his back in the middle of the floor. The farmer laughed and bought the TV.

One day Dad encountered Cousin Richard, who had a black eye and a cut on his cheek. "What happened to you?" Dad wanted to know.

"Oh, my wife was in the shower, and I saw the plunger in the corner of the bathroom. I just grabbed that thing and whacked it right on her butt, whap. Darned thing stuck. Funniest thing I ever did see. Couldn't stop laughing. And she was trying to pull it off. It really was stuck tight, her butt being wet and all. Well, she tugged and tugged, and I just kept laughing. Well, by the time she got it loose, she was really pissed off. Sheila beat the hell out of me with that damned plunger. My eye hurts, and I laugh every time I think of her with that plunger on her butt."

In a town like New London, if somebody wrote a bad check, all the merchants told each other the same morning. If something was stolen, somehow everybody had a good notion of who did it. When the safe was stolen from the school, everyone figured Billy Gould did it. So the sheriff goes to Billy's house, says, "Fred, I gotta talk to Billy." And he says, "Bill, the safe was taken from the school last night. Did you do it?" And Billy is quiet for a bit, then he says, "Yeah, me and Merle White did it." Fred had to buy a new safe, and Billy and Merle had to pay back the $25 in cash they got.

Up the road from New London, in Perry, a couple of tires were stolen from the post office. Robbing a U.S. Post Office is a federal crime, and the FBI investigates. The agents just drove around until they found someone with a new pair of tires. Everything is easily visible in a small town.

The Fall of '57

The idea of going to high school in Hannibal had excited me. With a population of ten thousand, Hannibal had always seemed like a city, a real city with a public library in a handsome brick building, a bus system, even parking meters. Hannibal High's student body of seven hundred and fifty was a number approaching New London's entire population of eight hundred thirty-seven. My class in New London High School numbered eleven.

I walked down the terrazzo-floored hallway that first school day in the fall of 1957 with both anxiety and high expectations. The auditorium had fixed seats just like in a movie theater. The broad green lawn, the stately high-fired brick building looked like a university to me. Surely the students would be more sophisticated, polite, mature, interested in the arts. But it turns out that people from one Missouri town are pretty much like people in the next Missouri town.

The students on average were probably no worse and certainly no better. Lacking in grace, ever critical, I appointed myself an arbiter of good taste and proper behavior. In this role I let someone know that his conduct was crude. This observation went through the student body like wildfire. "Crude" was such an odd word. It gained currency and entered the student body vocabulary. Many things became crude, and students would ask me, somewhat mockingly, if I thought a particular activity or person might be crude. It was mostly good-natured, and I took it as such.

In English class one day, Miss Fetty read a poem and commented that one of her students had been moved to tears by that particular poem. John Berger, from the back of the room, said, "That was Baylis." The class roared with laughter. I thought it was funny, too.

It was in the physical ed class that my attitude was more problematic. I hated sports at this time in my life, did not have a competitive spirit. I believed in the motto emblazoned on the auditorium proscenium: "It matters not whether you won or lost but how you played the game"—Grantland Rice. So when we played touch football, I really didn't give a damn where the ball actually was "down." To me it was about exercise, running around. I participated because it was required, but I remained aloof and slightly bemused. This was, of course, a sin that would be punished. Where the ball was down turned out to be a matter of great importance. There were arguments, there was shouting. I made a dismissive comment, something like, "Who cares where the ball is down. Here, there. It doesn't matter."

I had so underestimated how much it mattered, how much Buddy King cared. How much passion and emotion was invested. So I was unprepared for the fist that Buddy planted firmly in the middle of my face. Buddy was the football team quarterback, outweighed me by fifty pounds, all muscle. He could walk into a bar and order a drink without being carded. We tussled for a minute or so, but it was over almost immediately. And because Buddy was basically a good guy, albeit hot-tempered, he apologized as I stood dazed and bleeding. Dad came to school and took me to see

Dr. Smith, the ear, nose, and throat specialist. "Broken like an egg hit with a spoon," he said of my nose. But that was all. You can't put a cast on a nose.

That was on a Thursday. On Friday, Boyce Embry threw a carton of milk across the cafeteria at me. Boyce had a large, cylindrical body with arms like huge sausages. His expressionless eyes were hooded by a single eyebrow. My only previous encounter with him had been four years earlier when he had attempted to drown me in a Y swimming class. I felt like a loser then, and I felt like a loser again that Friday.

Friday night was the homecoming dance. I had a date with Jeanne, a clarinet player with curly brown hair. She was a year older than me. We had met during summer band practice the year before, and she had asked me to go out with her to a church hayride. I liked her, but her feelings about me seemed more conditional. We were double-dating with her friend Carol and the first horn player and would ride in his family's classy new DeSoto. I talked as though I had a cold: my nasal passages were swollen closed. She handled all this pretty well, but she was embarrassed by the whole thing, upper classman that she was. It would be a while before she would go out with me again.

The conflict with Raymond began in the locker room. There are things you don't share, and your deodorant stick is one of them. I emerged from the shower to find Raymond using mine. I felt my territory had been invaded. I was astonished by Raymond's boorishness and said so. He pretended not to understand why I was offended. The confrontation was threatening, and I felt scared.

153

As the weather got colder, PE class moved into the gym for basketball, yet another game I did not play well. I couldn't dribble, throw straight, or make a free throw. When the ball came into my hands, I was lost. Everything moved too fast. I abhorred sweat and loathed physical contact. It was in this context that Raymond began to foul me mercilessly at every possible opportunity—even when I didn't have the ball. Phys ed became my hell, Raymond my tormentor. In his effort to humiliate me and provoke a fight, he finally knocked me to the floor. I didn't want to fight, and I couldn't figure out what was going on with him. Buddy King tried to mediate, to no avail. Raymond announced that at the next class, he was going to mop the floor with me. In the locker room I shook so intensely that I could barely tie my shoes.

At band practice after lunch, I trembled as I took my horn from the case. Everyone in the entire school knew that my ritual sacrifice would take place the next day. I tried to make light of it. As the band members were taking their seats and beginning to warm up, Bobby Parsons, the first chair trumpet player, took me aside. A year my senior, Bobby put an arm around my shoulder and spoke my name in an avuncular manner that took me completely by surprise. He put his horn in its case and stood facing me.

"Here's what you're gonna have to do," he said. "You grab him by the collar with one hand and hit him the face with the other, like this." And he demonstrated the move, gently grabbing my shirt collar and slowly going through the motions. I think he was half joking. But I took him seriously. Any battle plan was better than none.

I began to obsessively rehearse in my mind the simple motions Bobby had shown me. As I approached the feed-box before milking the cow, I reviewed the choreography. Right hand: grab collar. Left hand: make fist, cross, hit. It had rhythm and structure, like music. I understood music. I understood how to learn difficult fingering for a musical phrase. Repetition. So I did it again and again. As I walked back from the barn with the bucket of milk, I put the bucket down every dozen steps to practice. I even went over it as I put on my pajamas.

The next morning I had to get up and milk the cow. Oppressed with dread, I rehearsed the moves. As I dressed for school, I trembled through the motions. It was the fourth-period health class that Raymond had designated as the scene of my demise. I endured homeroom, English, algebra, and social studies, quaking like my aging and palsied Uncle Rec. I walked down the hallway with my heart pounding. Adrenaline seared my blood. I feared for my life.

As I approached the fourth-period classroom, Raymond was standing in the doorway waiting for me. Guys were standing along the wall leaning casually to watch. Others stood inside the classroom. Nobody wanted to miss the main event of the day. I didn't know what I expected. I can't imagine what he expected. Perhaps he thought I was so scared that I simply wouldn't show, coward that I was. But there he stood, with an armload of books and wearing glasses. I would have to wait for him to remove them. Maybe he didn't really want to fight after all. But he had to. He had announced his intention and had refused Buddy

King's offer to arbitrate. And he was blocking my entry into the classroom.

Trembling like a leaf in a breeze, I attempted to walk around him on his right. But he moved to the right. I tried to walk around him on his left. Again he blocked my way. I was on the verge of tears. There was no way around.

There was no sound. My right hand grabbed Raymond's collar, twisting it. My left hand formed a fist as I pulled it back to my shoulder, my body turning to force it toward Raymond's face. He had scared me almost to death. I was fighting for my life. I was a tight-wound spring let loose. I shredded Raymond's shirt. Holding his hair, I banged his head on the floor, smashing his glasses. I fought like a girl as everyone in the room watched in silence, amazed. I used every resource at my command. I would have bitten him if I had thought of it.

When the coach came in and broke it up, Raymond was shirtless. His upper lip was bleeding; his books and fragments of his glasses were all over the floor. I was almost untouched. But my heart was raging as though it might jump out of my chest. I have no idea what happened in the class that followed.

When I entered the cafeteria for lunch, I received a standing ovation. Boyce Embry would never again, giant that he was, throw a milk carton at me. Nor would any student lay a hand on me in aggression. I had destroyed my image as a wimp.

The next week, Raymond said I owed him ten dollars for his broken glasses. I told him I felt bad about that but never paid him.

I did make friends and had a social life at Hannibal High. Jeanne went with me to Ward Smith's New Year's eve party. I found it impressive that Ward's table had five kinds of cheese. I had known of only cheddar and Velveeta. My world was expanding. I bought a racket and went out for tennis. In the yearbook, I'm in the team picture even though I never did learn to play. I just couldn't make sense of the scoring system.

Uncle Harry's Gone

The phone call from my brother John was to the point: "Looks like Uncle Harry died." Jim's email didn't say much else. "Kelly found him. Oh, Jim doesn't want you to call Mom. She doesn't know yet. He wants us to let Kelly tell her. That's all. I got to be somewhere. Goodbye."

I should have known he would die sometime. But he was only eighty-seven. I'd been thinking I should give him a call, see how he was doing. He would have been surprised to hear from me. Probably would have thought it a bit strange. Mostly because I'd never called him before. But he had a phone, so it would have been possible.

Uncle Harry was a bachelor, lived with Grandma Ruby for her last forty years. She lived to be just a month shy of ninety-nine. She'd had a colostomy when she was in her late forties. So the last few years of care may have been a bit demanding, taking care of that colostomy bag. Maybe not—Grandma Ruby was not one to make a fuss. But the last time I visited Grandma, you could smell that colostomy bag. Wasn't pretty.

I was probably eleven or twelve the summer I helped Uncle Harry build a fence on our farm. I wasn't all that useful, but I was somebody to talk to. Uncle Harry never seemed to have any interest in girls, or women, for that matter. Not like Uncle Rec, who liked to sit with Mae Reilley on her front porch there across from the Christian Church. Uncle Harry was a nice enough fellow, though. Just seemed to prefer the company of men. Summer evenings he'd sit with four or five other bachelors on the low concrete block wall at the DX gas station across from the post office and catty-corner from the telephone office.

"We call it pressing concrete," he said. "Every once in a while somebody'll drive past. Then we'll say something. Not much to talk about unless something's happened. Like the time your Uncle Otis stopped out on the farm-to-market road with engine trouble. Checked to see if there was water in the battery, and the damned battery blew up in his face. Got battery acid in both eyes. For darned certain, Otis would have lost his sight if Doc Chris hadn't come by. Threw baking soda in his eyes. Neutralized the acid. Bad luck followed by some really good luck. That was really something. Most of the time we just sit there. Every so often a truck will come through on the way to St. Louis, stop at the light, and move on. Once in a while somebody'll get a Coke out of the machine. If anybody has some whis-key, we pass it around."

We were putting in a new woven-wire fence with a strand of barbed wire on top. All the postholes had to be dug by hand with a pair of posthole diggers. Fact was, Uncle Harry did most of the work. Besides, Dad wasn't paying me to help. I was most interested in the war. Uncle Harry had been in the Philippines.

"When we were pulling out, the sergeant was supposed to sell things we didn't need anymore. No point shipping stuff back to the USA. He had to get rid of a military truck. Several locals wanted it. He said he needed one hundred dollars. Couldn't take a penny less. Nobody had a hundred dollars. So the sergeant put a tin of canned heat on the engine. Melted right down through the block. Sarge said, 'Had to get what it was worth. Couldn't give away U.S. Army assets.' Poor damned Filipinos just stood there and watched, couldn't believe their eyes. Would have made good use of a truck like that. After we had boarded ship, before leaving port, there were two local boats with women on them came alongside. Men on the boats were charging a dollar to do the women, right there on the deck. Must have been a hundred guys climbed down there to do it. Right out in the open. Not me. No sir-ree.

"Back in the States, as I was walking past a barracks one afternoon, somebody yelled, 'I said, 'Turn off the god-damned lights!' There were five quick shots. Bang, bang, bang, bang, bang. Just like that. Then the guy yelled 'When I say turn off the god-damned lights, I mean turn off the lights.' Then it was quiet, like nothing had happened."

I didn't know what to make of Uncle Harry's war. Uncle Harry's war wasn't at all like the movie *Bataan*, with soldiers walking through the jungle being picked off one by one. No mention of landing on beaches. Grandma had a picture of him in uniform on her dresser. But it seemed like he never touched a gun. Never did any shooting. Actually, Uncle Harry was a mild and dependable person, a blue-collar man. Seemed to have done a lot of different things. Always paid cash.

He said, "I went to the wrestling matches down at the Armory in Hannibal with Charley Silvey. We were sitting in the crowd up on the bleachers. Charley offered me a drink of whiskey. I said, 'Heck no, everybody will see me.' Charley said, 'Close your eyes.'"

I finally called Mom. She said, "No point in coming back for the funeral. All that travel for just a few minutes' visitation in the funeral home and the service at ten a.m. Then we drive to Frankford for the burial. Our preacher, Reverend Day, will be doing the service. If they had the service at the church, women of the church would have served dinner. He's going to be buried next to Mom and Pop. We got his plot for real cheap. I think it's in the road."

Dias's Brother and Benny Letcher

Whenever I call home to keep in touch with Mom,
I get an update on who's died back in New London.
Almost always somebody's died or is really sick. Maybe
because the community is small, and Mom worked at the
post office, so she knows everybody in town, all eight
hundred and thirty-seven. And sort of knows almost
everybody in the county, all four thousand of them.
And people are always doing foolish things back there.
So Mom asks me if I know Mrs. Hutchins, the county
registrar.

"No, Mom, I don't."

"Well, she pulled out onto Highway 61 right in front
of a big trailer truck. Was killed instantly. We don't know
what she was thinking about. She was driving across the
highway to go west on that farm-to-market road. She must
have looked down at something on the front seat or maybe
she had something on her mind. She was such a nice person
and everybody liked her."

"l didn't know her, Mom."

"Well, she was real popular. And I wonder if you ever
knew Dias Keith's brother."

"I didn't know he had one."

"Well, his brother was on the faculty over at the university, and he had a son. The boy had been in Vietnam and
had a drinking problem. And the father would have to go
several times each week and bring him back from the bar.
And Dias's brother had been married, too. The woman

162

lived in Seattle, and she had a daughter. Anyway, the daughter went over to Columbia, and she called the house, and the boy agreed to meet her and take her out to dinner. Well, the boy acted real strange during dinner. Said he loved the girl. Must be his half-sister. And gave her his dad's diamond ring. Well, she called her mom out in Seattle and said how strange it all was. And the mother called the sheriff back in Columbia and said he'd better look into the matter, that something strange was going on. Well, the sheriff went to Dias's brother's house and found him sitting at the dining room table. Been sittin' there for two days, dead as a doornail. Been shot in the side and in the neck. The son was there in the house. Pretty much like nothin' had happened. The sheriff asked if he'd shot his father, and he said, yes he had. Just like that. He'd completely flipped his lid.

"Dias had to go over and make funeral arrangements. Your brother Jim drove him around, introduced him to an attorney to take care of the estate. I went to the funeral with a few of my friends. It was so sad. The son wasn't there— he was in jail.

"Last night I hosted the Circle. There were seventeen of us here. We held the meeting in the living room and I served cake and punch in the family room. Everybody had a good time."

That's the way phone calls with Mom are, there's always something. But everything, whether it's a carry-in dinner at the church or a murder, it's reported with the same gravity. And then I told Mom I had called Benny Letcher, as she had suggested.

"Benny said he had moved to Uncle Rex's farm when he was eight years old. They'd lived in the big white house. That was Uncle Rex's house."

"Yeah," says Mom, "Uncle Rex lived with Granddad and Grandma, slept on a cot in the dining room in the winter and in the basement in summer. This very house you grew up in. The house was only three rooms back then."

So I told Mom about the conversation with Benny and how Dorothy got on the phone, too, and they both seemed happy to hear from one of Dad's boys. I asked about what they did, Dad and Benny.

"Oh, we went to the movies together," Benny said. "We was both eight years old and we played together every day. We really had fun. We'd ride the horses and try to do the tricks we'd seen Tom Mix do in the movie. Once when Ed and me both rode on the same horse, he tried to dump me off, but I held onto him and we both fell off. We laughed to high heaven.

"Your grandfather had lots of horses. He used to carry the mail, with the horse and buggy. And Ed and me, we'd ride 'em all over those two farms. And your Aunt Lucy Frances, too. Oh, we had a good time. There wasn't anything we wouldn't try. And your dad had a little donkey. Stubborn thing. We'd use a buggy bridle on it. Had a strap, went from the top of his head to the saddle so he'd have to hold his head up. If he couldn't get his head down, he couldn't buck, and you could stay on him. Otherwise he'd throw you off every time."

Benny said he and Dad worked on the farm together as they got older. And then they worked for the railroad.

I told Mom all this, and she said Dad and Benny had always stayed in touch.

"He always came by to see us whenever he came back to town. And when we were in Denver on that trip west in 1948, we visited Benny and Dorothy. They had a nice neat home and the children were very quiet. Benny always had two full-time jobs and sent every one of his kids to college. Benny's colored, you know. His wife was an Allison. Her family didn't approve of Benny. They thought he was too much of a lady's man. So when he and Dorothy decided to get married, they had to elope. They got a marriage license and had the minister at our church marry them the same afternoon and then headed off to Kansas City right after the marriage ceremony. Her family was really teed off. They're such fine people."

Then Mom told me about Dad.

"He's doing as well as you could expect for a person who's had a stroke. I try to drive down to see him for a while every day. He's still got that sore on his foot. It isn't healing very fast. Sometimes your dad's in a good mood, sometimes he isn't. Sometimes he seems to be aware of what's going on around him, and sometimes he's just in his own world. I told him with all the rain we'd been having, there was some mud seeping into the basement. He said you'd expect to have mud when you have rain."

Chicago

I see myself as the twelve-year-old boy I was then. Sitting stiffly on the train looking out the window and thinking about the experience before me. It is summer, and I am wearing a starched and ironed short-sleeved shirt, seersucker pants. My weekend clothes are in a small suitcase in the overhead rack. As always, I feel slightly out of place. I'm going to Chicago to visit my half-brother Steve. He just finished high school and has a summer job in the big city.

Steve has always seemed a bit privileged. Spending his summer vacations with our grandparents, his school year with his mother in Bowling Green, thirty miles away. In the Bowling Green High School Band he played the tuba. And he was on the basketball team. Dad is proud of him. Steve is good-natured, loves to tell stories about himself and his friends. Over the years we played with toys in the sand pile, climbed in the hayloft, walked in the woods together, read comics in the basement of Grandma's house on rainy days.

As far as I can determine, now that he is grown up, Steve has only two real interests: cars and girls. For several years now he has been almost completely preoccupied with sex. He talks a lot about girls and things he has done on dates. He once told me that he is so horny he'd fuck a snake if I'd hold it. On a recent date he had spent the entire night trying to seduce a reluctant girl. But, when she finally was willing, he had gone soft. "It was like trying to get a clam into a slot machine," he says.

Steve is going to show me Chicago.

I had wild sexual fantasies, playing out my anxieties toward the opposite sex. I wanted some kind of contact so much. But I had so little in the way of a model for that relationship that I could only have the most bizarre kind of fantasy. If any situation came about that brought me close to a girl, I could only retreat and become embarrassed. I played in the hayloft once with Joyce, who lived down the road from us, and wanted so much to touch her. I think she might have been receptive to me. But in those moments, I could only be aware of how inexperienced and full of fear I was, even the certainty that I would be rejected. I was actually certain that if I tried to touch her, she would scream and her father would come and I would be disgraced forever.

Now, I am thinking about Jolene, a girl my age who lives in Chicago. I have her address and phone number in my pocket, and I plan to visit her. We were in the first and second grades together. When her dad's Kaiser-Frazer dealership went out of business, her family moved to Chicago, where Joe got work as a truck driver. Jolene and her mother, Faye, are both blond and look exactly like the women who pose for pictures in magazine ads. Sometimes I would just sit and gaze at Jolene, she was so pretty.

I had gotten her attention on my first day of school by kicking her and leaving a mark on her starched yellow cotton skirt. She told on me, and Miss Christine said, "Young man, you march right up here and apologize to Jolene." I was dreadfully embarrassed.

I know in my heart that girls and I have some kind of sexual compatibility. I have seen the animals coupling all over the farm. But I have no clear idea how it actually works with people. Even seeing Olive Oyl and Popeye coupled on the page of an eight-page bible that one of the Lake boys had brought to school didn't really explain anything. A little girl lifted her skirt at church one Sunday, and I felt compelled to go tell her mother that the child didn't have any underwear on. I had wanted to look at the child, inspect her. But that was in Sunday school.

But now I was going to Chicago. Jolene would be there, and my waking dream is to visit her in her home. She will be there alone. And I am filled with anticipation, a dark hope that something might transpire between us. Something blatantly sexual, and I have no idea how this can come about. What could precipitate a coupling? I can envision the goal. I have the phone number and the address. But the prospect also fills me with a certain dread. The darkness of it all. This unspeakably forbidden desire. Already I am filled with conflict and guilt.

One cold winter morning, when I was about four years old, I stood over the heat outlet in the floor, the warm air rising around me. Mom making cinnamon toast in the electric oven. Coating slices of bread with thick, fresh cream, sugar, sprinkling cinnamon. I am still wearing my pajamas and my penis stands out with an early morning stiffness and I fondle it, mostly because it's there, attached to me, and notice that it feels good. And Mom looks right at me and says, "You're not supposed to do that. It's not nice to play with yourself that way." And she gives me that certain look that she has. It is a don't-do-that look, with her head turned slightly away, but the eyes are looking straight at me. Her lips are pursed and her cheeks are sucked in. Everything about her in this moment says "don't do that, especially if it feels good." She doesn't explain herself.

Through the window of the train I gaze down the long rows of corn in the Illinois fields. Green and Green tractors move in the distance like colorful bugs. I know what it is to travel repeatedly the length of a cornfield. Steering carefully, watching the dark earth break and crumble up around the roots of the cornstalks for hours on end. Stopping occasionally at the end of the field for a drink of water. Taking a few minutes to rest in the shade. Watching a ladybug crawl up my arm. In the distance, the call of a meadowlark and rhythmic chuffing of the John Deere on Albert Boss's farm. That is the world I know. Tractors and cows, fields of corn, bales of alfalfa.

As the train passes through Burlington, Iowa, I notice a large sign painted on the brick wall of a building announcing that this is the site for the first use of the Westinghouse air brake. And I am thinking that there's probably a diagram in the *World Book Encyclopedia* showing how it works.

One thing I am looking forward to in Chicago is the radio station that plays classical music. John Croll told me about it. I am drawn to this music even though there is none in my life except on the radio. Since my earliest years, listening to the opening music to the "Lone Ranger" and "Sgt. Preston of the Yukon" excited and awakened me. The haunting theme from Grofé's Grand Canyon Suite with someone named Johnny shouting out, "Call for Phillip Morris." I savored every second of those music fragments.

And I have discovered that on Sunday afternoons, there is a New York Philharmonic concert I can get on the car radio. I listen lying down on the wide front seat of the Hudson.

The train arrives in Chicago in the early afternoon. Bill Holliday, one of Steve's roommates, meets me at the station, explaining that Steve can't get away from his work. Bill is from New London. He's selling Ford cars. He drives me in the '53 Ford demonstrator. I am amazed by the deafening noise of the downtown street. "They call those trains up there the el, " he says. "Short for elevated." He leaves me at the apartment. "Steve will be back around 5:30. Make yourself comfortable."

The apartment is dingy and dark. The towels in the bathroom smell of mildew. It's depressing. Everything is a mess. I decide there is nothing to do but clean the place. I make the beds. Locate the landlady and borrow a vacuum sweeper and vacuum the entire apartment. I find a suitable rag and dust the furniture. There is a small AM radio, and I tune in the classical music station. Throughout the whole afternoon every selection played is completely new and strange. I would be so happy to hear a Sousa march or the William Tell overture or Beethoven's Fifth Symphony. But the Chopin and Scriabin are difficult and challenging. The reception is poor and full of static. I listen carefully and without joy.

At length Steve gets back from work, with Bob German, his other roommate. Bob's dad runs the dry cleaner in New London. My first night of big city life features hot dogs and stock car racing. I am rooting for the Hudson mostly because Dad has one. The Hudson dealership in Hannibal displays posters that show Hudson's winning stock car races, with checkered flags everywhere. So I am expecting the Hudson to win. But it doesn't.

Saturday we visit the aquarium and go for a swim in Lake Michigan. Saturday night we go with Bob and Bill to the Chicago Theater, a gigantic movie palace. The curtain rises, and a big band is on stage, and there are acrobats and then the highlight of the evening: the Four Crew Cuts in person singing their top 40 hit, "Shaboom, shaboom. Ya, dada dah, dada dah" and so on. The audience goes completely wild. I actually like "Sha-boom," and I'm having a good time.

Then comes the movie, *The High and the Mighty*, in Vista Vision. That impresses me because I've just read an article about Vista Vision in *Popular Science*. The screen is gigantic, and John Wayne plays an airline pilot. The plane is heading for Hawaii and is leaking fuel. They can't turn back. He's not sure the plane will make it. And there's a woman passenger who is going to meet somebody and she's crying a lot because she's not sure he will still love her. Her mascara is running and her fake eyelashes are coming off. And I really hate fake eyelashes and mascara. Knowing how my mother would disapprove, certain that if God wanted you to have dark eyelashes, he would have given them to you.

On Sunday we're headed for Maxwell Street. Bill says, "You can get terrific bargains on Maxwell Street." Steve says, "Yeah, but you have to watch out 'cause they're all Jews, out there." Bill says, "I'm not sure they're all Jews.

Some of 'em are just foreigners." And Steve says, "Jews, foreigners, they're all the same. You have to watch out."

We walk down the street and I have never seen anything like it. People are actually selling things from carts, right out on the sidewalk even. It feels like another country. The people speak with strange accents. Steve buys a bundle of ten pairs of work socks for a dollar. They seem awfully thin to me. Bill buys a pair of slacks with gaudy saddle stitching down the side seams. He says he will remove the saddle stitching and have a decent pair of pants for cheap. But when we got back to the apartment, he inspects the pants more closely and finds that it is the saddle stitching that holds the pants together. He is really pissed off.

It is Monday, my last day in Chicago, and I am going to visit Jolene. I board a city bus. I am full of apprehension. I will have to change buses and ask the driver to let me know where I will have to get off. It is all so strange. The trip seems to last forever. We go through a region where the air is so bad I think I am going to suffocate. There is haze and the sky is overcast. The air is a bit cold and I am in short sleeves. When I get off the bus, I am hungry and disoriented. I am lost. I stand on the street trying to get my bearings and decide to ask for directions in the bar just down the street a few doors. It seems so incredibly forbidding. The front window is painted opaque so you can't see inside. I enter the dark room with caution in my step. Three men are playing pool. The bartender is talking to a couple. He turns to me and says,

"What da ya want, baby?" He is thick, tough-looking with a crewcut.

"I need some directions," I say. He wants to know how old I am and where I come from. I ask to buy a bag of corn puffs and he wants to know how much money I have. "A dollar," I say. He gives me the corn puffs and won't accept my quarter. I really have more money, I say, but that I'm not supposed to say how much. Still he refuses any payment. I thank him and exit the bar feeling crummy and confused. Ashamed to have lied about the money.

I walk the six blocks to the address I have for Jolene's house. I am astonished to find how small it is. Dark cinder bricks with a white wood door. The day is overcast and dull, devoid of color. I stand on the small concrete platform that serves as a porch with deep misgivings. My hope of seeing a childhood friend. My dark agenda. Is this the right house? Maybe I should just go back, not even knock on the door. What will I say?

I knock on the door. There is no response. I had imagined embracing Jolene. On the train I had imagined her serving me a coke, and we would talk, and somehow, we would become intimate. I knock on the door again. No response. Perhaps she's in the bathroom. Maybe actually taking a bath. Maybe if I persist a bit longer she will appear. She'll be wrapped in a towel. Maybe she'll be completely naked. I knock again. And there's a voice from behind the door.

"Who is it?" It's a woman's voice, not Jolene's.

"Is this the Mitchell residence?"

And the woman's voice says, "It is. What do you want?"

I tell the woman who I am. And the door begins to unlock.

"Oh, my goodness," she says as the door springs open. "Ed and Sarah's little boy. My goodness, let me take a look at you."

It's Faye, Jolene's mother. She's dressed in a housecoat and seems happy to see me.

"Come right on in. How did you get here, and what are you doing is Chicago? How are Ed and Sarah?"

"Oh, good." I say.

"And your little brothers? What a surprise to see you. Well it's lucky I didn't feel so good and decided to stay home today. I'm feeling better now, but I felt just awful this morning." She does look a bit frazzled, like she's been sleeping in that chenille bathrobe.

"Where's Jolene?" I ask.

"She left for Missouri yesterday. She'll be in New London to stay a few days with her aunt next week. She's gonna be real surprised when she finds out you came all the way here to call on her. Well, I bet you're hungry. Come on into the kitchen and I'll fix you something to eat."

"I'm OK," I say. But she insists. I follow her into the kitchen and listen to her while she slices a tomato and puts some lunch meat on a couple of slices of Wonder bread, slathers it with Miracle Whip. "Would you like a Pepsi? Hun?" And I say that would be fine and she pours one for herself too and sits down opposite me. She asks me about a whole bunch of people back in New London, and I tell her everybody's O.K.

"You know I miss that little town and all those nice people. It's a real special place." I'm wondering what's so special about it, but I say, "Yeah, small towns are special."

"You still taking piano lessons from Mrs. Crockett?"

"No" I say, "Mrs. Crockett died three years ago."

"My goodness," Faye says. "Well, she was old, wasn't she? Jolene used to tell me that Mrs. Crockett wore a housecoat and her husband's socks while giving piano lessons."

And I say, "Yes she did. She pushed my fingers down onto the keys with the point of her pencil when I hit the wrong note."

Faye laughs and says, "I remember the time you kissed Jolene right out there in front of everybody after she played a piano solo at Sunday school. What were you thinking of, young man?" And she laughs again as I turn crimson. "And in the second grade you put a wind-up toy down the back of her dress. You were a little devil, I'd say. But you know Joe and I both thought the world of Ed and Sarah. We thought you were kind of a spirited boy. I think boys should be spirited."

On the bus back, I am holding the wallet-size photo of Jolene that Fay has given me. Jolene is even prettier now that she is twelve. I burp a big Pepsi burp and imagine lying on top of Jolene on the burgundy velour sofa of her own living room in the house I have just left. The living room with the twelve-inch television, the heart-shaped planter with the philodendron.

A week later Jolene is at Sunday school. I muster the courage to say, "Hello." She is a head taller than me, which only adds to my feelings of inadequacy. She is almost a woman and I still look like a boy. She wears elaborate makeup. Mom doesn't approve of makeup on young girls, so neither do I. And she says, "Hi," but there's a cold aloofness in her voice. I tell her about my trip, and she says she got a letter from her mom about my visit.

"Mom was real happy to see you." Jolene speaks with a lisp, which I had forgotten. She talks to Mom and says she has made the suit she is wearing, from pillow ticking. Mom thinks this is very creative and admires it even though I know Mom is thinking this girl is wearing too much makeup. And I know this is the end of my imaginary love affair with Jolene. She's too tall, and I can tell she doesn't like me.

In spite of the dinginess and the noise, there is something about the city that excites me, calls out to me, even as it repels me. I know this when, as I walk toward the barn lot to milk the cows, the fumes of a diesel bus passing on the highway waft over the fence to my nostrils. The smell of the bus fumes is sweet and fills me with longing.

Walking on the Farm

I remember thinking while walking about on the farm.
Many of the tasks required minimal attention, leaving much
of the mind vacant for dreaming and wondering. And that
is what I did throughout my youth. I wondered at the late
afternoon light of early autumn and winter. Light in marvel-
ous shades of orange, umber, red, and gold. Light shaped
and shaded by laces of high cloud layers. Light that filled
me with wonder and a feeling of richness.

I can remember walking home from the barn with a
small pail of milk and playing the most magnificent game
with myself. I imagined that the scale of everything was
different and that the end of a stick I carried in my hand
was a train traveling the hills and valleys of the ground
before my steps. So fascinated was I in this journey that I
did not walk in a straight line but wandered in a compli-
cated and labyrinthine course. In my child's vision, I
saw rich landscapes in the sparkling snow, which now
covered the ground like the butter icing of a white cake. I
thought that I would let all the children in the world ride
my train. I did not even think of myself in a particular
role on that train. I simply thought of the job of looking
out from its windows as it crossed dozens and dozens
of bridged valleys and gorges. There would have been
no factor considered in making the route of my railroad
except that it should be as beautiful as it could be. I
wanted life to be beautiful. I was still young and certain
that it could be so.

On another walk when I was several years older, I went through the woods. It was late afternoon in the spring on a school day. I was looking at the small things that grew at the edges of the trees and was amazed to see that there were so many kinds of moss and tiny grasses. Each seemed rich and full of fascination, a whole other world there at my fingertips, and I wanted eagerly to slide into it or bring it into mine. The latter I attempted by carefully taking a sample of each to carry home with me.

I had imagined that I might create a tiny world of my own design so that I could always look into it, live in it with my mind, and look out from it. I placed the little patches of vegetation on a large slab of marble we had on the back porch. Because I did not water my collection, it died. I did not obtain any wisdom from that experience at the time. I merely felt deeply the disappointment of not being able to make my little dream real.

I can't imagine what might have made me speculate on it, but I remember considering how the stars and planets might have an influence on my life. I could see very little relationship between them and myself. It did occur to me that radiation from a star might do something powerful. X-rays, gamma rays, or some other more obscure energy. I did not think of tides pulled by the moon. I did not even think of the light from the sun. I just thought of the stars.

It is curious that my first child was born with a birth defect that could have been caused by a particle of energy striking the twenty-first chromosome in the zygote. I don't know that there is even the slightest bit of empirical data for this. But it still might be so.

Walking on the Farm

I often dreamed while riding the tractor. I was plowing a field on the north edge of our farm, the field bordering Albert Boss's land. To plow is to drive the tractor back and forth the length of the field, keeping a fix on the furrow that was turned over on the previous round. Your ears are full of the tractor engine. You feel the heat of the sun on your face, the vibration and jerking of the machine under your feet. Sometimes you sit on the metal seat and sometimes you stand as at the wheel of a steamship. As you make the trips across the field, you smell the fumes of the engine and the moist fragrance of the freshly turned soil. Sweat drips down your side, and your mouth turns dry. But your imagination is free to roam as mine did. Still, there was always the present moment, the fence line, the trees along the railroad track, the nest of meadowlark eggs just overturned and covered with turf, the occasional snake cut in half by the plow, the hawk high overhead.

At the end of the field on one such plowing day, I stopped the engine, got down off the red tractor with its lowly two-bottom plow, and walked two hundred yards to the three-room house that sat among elm trees at the end of the small gravel road that bordered our farm on the east. I knocked on the door and asked for a drink of water. The old man who lived there brought me a glass of water and we talked for a spell. The man was probably in his seventies, thin and weathered-looking, said he had been injured by mustard gas in World War I. He was still suffering from it, he said. Still felt it in his legs and lungs. He talked about things he remembered, but they didn't mean enough to stay with me.

As I was about to leave he said, "Wait a minute." He went back into the house and came back with a small blue softback book, the operating manual for a metal lathe. He said he knew all about that lathe, became a machinist after the war.

"I got no use for this manual anymore. Pretty much know it by heart. You might find it interesting. The drawings are real good. It's yours," he said, handing it to me. I thanked him, said I appreciated it. It felt special to receive a gift, coming as it did in the middle of the day when I hadn't expected a gift. I enjoyed talking to older folks. I had been taught to show respect to my elders. Mostly I did. And it felt good to sit in the shade for a spell, out of the sun. I asked for another glass of water, and we talked some more.

Both Mom and Dad were Roosevelt Democrats who had tasted the tough times of the Depression years and never forgot them. They were ordinary farm people, but also different. I have figured out that Mom was probably the smartest person in the county. Not the best educated, not the wisest, but somehow able to keep learning and keep going. Dad was an enigma, hard for me to read, full of darkness and misery, loyal to his friends and teachers, always respectful to his animals.

Living on the farm didn't feel like a gift, although I couldn't imagine living in a town. What could you do in a town? Play with other kids, I suppose. I didn't spend that much time in town. My years on the farm were all the years of my childhood, from the day I came home from the hospital with Mom until the day at the end of my second year of college when Dad drove me to St. Louis to begin my trip to California.

I look back on my life with a certain kind of awe. Not because my life had been wonderful, but because it had been miraculous. Not because of my wisdom or achievements. In fact, my life had been full of misery, mostly of my own making. And a certain amount of joy: pretty much the gift of others.

People jokingly say you can take the boy out of the farm, but you can't take the farm out of the boy. And it's true. Because in a certain sense, all of my life has been an attempt to make it in the real world that is not the farm, and all along I have remained that person I was at the moment I left that patch of ground in the heartland. I have remained optimistic in the face of failure and certain all the while that I could never really succeed in the ways that I had dreamed of.

Somehow everything that I am seems to have been coiled up and put into me on that farm: the sunlight of the bright summer days, the dreariness of winter storms, the kindness of strangers, and the ugliness of people who ought to have known better, the short-sightedness that kept me ignorant and the testosterone that made me arrogant, the warmth that made me capable of loving, the hurts that made me selfish and dangerous. Somehow, I read even my successes as variations of failure. I've managed to have some of each. And the seeds of it all were planted on that farm.

Acknowledgments

I gratefully acknowledge and thank the following individuals who have been influential in my life: Mom (Sarah Glascock); wife Katherine Glascock; brother John Glascock; William Mackie, whose idea to move from Missouri to Los Angeles gave me the same idea; Peter and Frances Yates, who employed and inspired me when I arrived in Los Angeles, and their son, John; Hardy Hanson, who suggested I make a film about Sister Corita Kent; Sister Corita herself, with her remarkable artwork and life example; Robert Snyder, with whom I made a number of films, and his wife, Allegra; Sy Wexler, in whose employment I was supported and inspired and for whom I made some more films, and his wife, Helen; Peter Pierce, another supporter, who taught at the then-named San Fernando Valley State College, and his wife; Roberta Goodwin, in whose writers group I began sharing my stories, and her husband, Archer; and the members of the Gene Stone Memorial Writers Group, with whom I have shared these and other tales for many years and whose friendship, feedback, and insights have helped to sustain me: Sam Eisenstein, Roberta Goodwin, Peter and Paula Tripodes, Birute Putrius Keblinskas, Lois Smith, Peter Cashorali, Alexandra Maeck, Codri Albenau, Torrey Burke, Mary Lou Cheyes, and Lulu Li.

About the Author

Baylis Glascock was born and raised on the family's
farm in New London, Missouri, ten miles from Hannibal,
where Mark Twain lived and wrote. It had been purchased
by his great-grandfather in 1875 with proceeds from the
Gold Rush. Baylis's stories are filled with Americana
that is folksy, funny, and at times heartbreaking. With a
sense of wonder and a wry wit, he explains his bafflement
with all things sexual and his equal confusion over racial,
ethnic, and economic disparity, realities that he treats with
sensitivity. After two years at the the University of Missouri,
Baylis moved to Los Angeles, where he took filmmaking
courses at USC and worked on projects for Walt Disney
Studios. Later he worked on numerous projects for several
studios as a filmmaker, editor, and director alongside Robert
Snyder, documenting Henry Miller and Buckminster Fuller,
and he made his own films of artist Sister Corita Kent. His
experimental film of the Watts Towers is preserved by the
Motion Picture Academy of Arts and Sciences.

Ingram Content Group UK Ltd.
Milton Keynes UK
UKHW010404010723
424377UK00006B/565